# Fiddle-Dee-Dee
## Songs, Stories & Activities

WITHDRAWN

**Jill Andrews & Linda Bair**

Alleyside Press

## Acknowledgements

Many thanks to the Alachua County Public Library System for providing incredible resources and services, our husbands for their suggestions and fortitude, and Linda's niece Laurie Edenfield, whose classroom experience and creativity provided a welcome resource when our wells went dry.

Published by Alleyside Press,
an imprint of Highsmith Press LLC
W5527 Highway 106
P.O. Box 800
Fort Atkinson, Wisconsin 53538-0800
**1-800-558-2110**

The paper used in this publication meets the minimum requirements of American National Standard for Information Science—Permanence of Paper for Printed Library Material. ANSI/NISO Z39.48

*Note regarding music selection:* All of the songs in this book have been identified as public domain music in either *Katzmarek's Encyclopedia of Public Domain Music* or the *Public Domain Report Music Bible: Volumes 1 and 2.* Lyrics by the authors are noted as additional lyrics or the original lyrics are provided beneath the score.

Johnson, Scott A., editor. *Public Domain Report Music Bible.* Vols. 1 & 2. Public Domain Research, 1996–1999.

*Katzmarek's Encyclopedia of Public Domain Music, Revised-Expanded.* Katzmarek Publishing, 1993.

# Contents

**Introduction**  5

**Animals**

1. *A-Hunting We Will Go*  6
2. *Animal Fair*  9
3. *Baa, Baa, Black Sheep*  13
4. *Barnyard Song*  16
5. *Blue Bird*  19
6. *Froggie Went A-Courtin'*  22
7. *Hickory, Dickory, Dock*  25
8. *Little Miss Muffet*  29
9. *My Pony*  31
10. *Shoo, Fly, Don't Bother Me*  34
11. *Three Little Kittens*  38
12. *Where Has My Little Dog Gone?*  41

**Mother Goose**

13. *A-Tisket, A-Tasket*  44
14. *Diddle, Diddle Dumpling*  47
15. *Fiddle-Dee-Dee*  51
16. *Hey Diddle Diddle*  53
17. *Humpty Dumpty*  56
18. *Jack and Jill*  59
19. *Little Jack Horner*  62
20. *Mary, Mary, Quite Contrary*  65
21. *The Muffin Man*  68
22. *Oh, Dear, What Can the Matter Be?*  71
23. *This Old Man*  74
24. *To Market, To Market*  77

**Moving Right Along**

25. *Did You Ever See a Lassie?*  81
26. *Lightly Row*  84
27. *London Bridge*  88
28. *Looby Loo*  91
29. *New River Train*  94
30. *Rig a Jig Jig*  98
31. *Rub-a-Dub-Dub*  101
32. *Sailing, Sailing*  103
33. *See-Saw, Margery Daw*  106
34. *She'll Be Comin' Round the Mountain*  109
35. *Skip to My Lou*  114
36. *The Teddy Bears' Picnic*  116

# Introduction

*Fiddle-Dee-Dee: Songs, Stories & Activities* is designed as a resource for the media center and primary classroom (kindergarten through second grade), but public libraries, preschools, and music programs will find that they can easily adapt the literature and activities to meet their specific programming needs.

This book is divided into three sections: Animals, Mother Goose, and Moving Right Along. Each section contains twelve nursery rhymes or folk songs which are the basis for a set of activities. The activities feature the song theme and include a list of selected picture books, crafts and art ideas, games, recipes and curriculum tie-ins.

The songs, books and activities can and should be adapted in any way that fits your programming needs. Books selected for the bibliographies can be replaced with your favorites or a title available in your library. While all books were chosen because of their wide availability in school and public libraries, many titles now go out of print very quickly, and may not be available for purchase. Of course, many wonderful new books are published each year, and you may wish to substitute one of these.

Preparation times are not given with activities, but all were chosen with ease of preparation in mind. You should find that most of the activities (but not all) require an average of fifteen minutes to complete. Some craft activities will require more time.

## A note on using music in programming

Many teachers and media specialists are very comfortable telling stories in their programs, but they dread the thought of including music. Perhaps you are one of them. Relax! You can incorporate music—even if you don't consider yourself musical. We think you will find that music gives you a new way to reach children, especially those who may not find success in regular academic pursuits. Gardner's theory of multiple intelligences lists the following intelligences: verbal/linguistic, logi-

cal/mathematical, visual/spatial, body/kinesthetic, musical/rhythmic, interpersonal, and intrapersonal. Musical activities incorporate all of these.

## Ideas for getting started

- If you don't feel comfortable singing:

    Buy or checkout one of the many commercial cassettes, CDs or videos.

    Ask someone (a music teacher?) to make a cassette tape for you.

    Ask for parent volunteers to come in to lead the singing—especially when first learning a song.

    Once the children know a song, ask one of the stronger singers to start the singing.

- As the class learns the songs, list them on a flip chart or on a poster.

- Have the kids illustrate the songs. Bind them into books for each child or for the classroom collection. Many of the songs lend themselves to "rewriting." Make up your own verses and put those into book form.

- Keep some instruments in the classroom (although this will probably depend on your tolerance for noise). Rhythm sticks, tambourines, and maracas are fun!

- When songs have many verses, consider making "prompt cards." (Example: "The Barnyard Song, p. 18)

- A great instrument for teachers is the autoharp. Ask your music teacher if there is one at the school (and if there is, ask for a quick lesson).

- Dramatize any of the songs or create your own games.

Most important: *Have fun!* You do **not** have to be a great singer. In fact, it is good for the children to see that you can enjoy music at any ability level.

# 1
# A-Hunting We Will Go

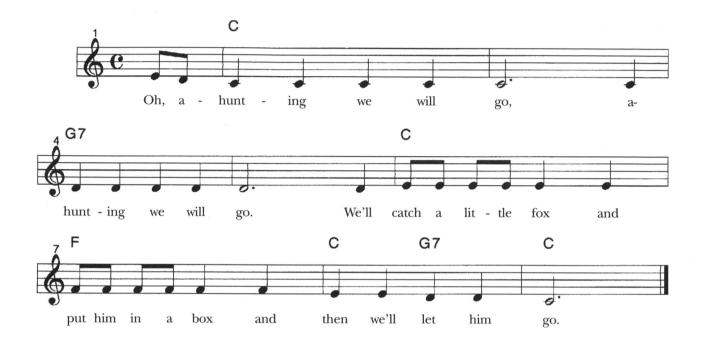

Oh, a - hunt - ing we will go, a-
hunt - ing we will go. We'll catch a lit - tle fox and
put him in a box and then we'll let him go.

# Programming Ideas

**Theme:** foxes

## Setting the Scene

Play a guessing game. Ask: "What animal am I thinking of?" Give hints like "big ears," "bright eyes," "sleek, shiny fur," "sharp teeth," "long, bushy tail," "likes to eat mice and chickens," and "rhymes with socks." Once the children have guessed "fox," ask them to tell you what they know about foxes.

## Song 🎵 *A-Hunting We Will Go*

Demonstrate movements to the song two or three times as you say or sing the words. (Make up your own or use the ones below). Ask a volunteer to come up and perform the movements for the class, then ask the class to try it. Sing the song four or five times with different volunteers coming to the front.

### Movements

Oh, a-hunting we will go,
(*put right hand to forehead and look to the right as if searching*)

A-hunting we will go,
(*put left hand to forehead and look to left as if searching*)

We'll catch a fox and
(*bend over to the ground and pretend to catch a fox*)

Put him in a box and
(*stand upright still pretending to hold the fox*)

Then we'll let him go.
(*pretend to release the fox*)

## Story 📖 *Grandfather Tang's Story*

After reading the story, hand out photocopies of the tangram pattern and the fox pattern on page 8. The children can color and cut the tangram and then paste it onto the fox pattern. Once they have pasted their tangram together, they can draw and color a background.

## Activities ✏️

### Research

Learn more about foxes by reading *Wild Dogs: Wolves, Coyotes, and Foxes*. As a class, write some of the facts on the board. This is an ideal opportunity for introducing or using a graphic organizer such as a web or diagram. Erase or hide the writing and quiz students informally with questions based on your reading.

### Dramatics

Read "The Ducks and the Fox" in *Fables*. Ask three children to act out the story creating their own dialogue.

### Problem Solving

Study the picture of the fox in *Quick as a Cricket*. The fox escaped the hunt. Ask: "If you were a fox, how would you escape?" As a class or in pairs, devise a way to escape. Encourage unorthodox thinking (ex. The fox persuades the little red hen to help. They make a sail and build a raft to sail down a river). Have children illustrate their escape plans and share them with the group.

### Music/Creative Writing

Ask: "What animal would you like to catch and keep for a little while? Why? How would you catch it? What would you keep it in?" Have children illustrate their ideas, then make up new verses for the song based on the answers.

## Books

Fox, Mem. *Hattie and the Fox*. Patricia Mullins, illustrator. Bradbury Press, 1987. A black hen spies a fox in the bushes, but the other animals are not concerned.

Hodge, Deborah. *Wild Dogs: Wolves, Coyotes and Foxes*. Pat Stephens, illustrator. Kids Can Press, 1997. Factual information and appealing illustrations of wild dogs.

Hutchins, Pat. *Rosie's Walk*. Macmillan, 1968. A hen escapes a luckless fox.

Lobel, Arnold. *Fables*. Harper & Row, 1980. A collection of original fables featuring animals.

Percy, Graham (illustrator). *The Cock, the Mouse, and the Little Red Hen*. Candlewick Press, 1992. The industrious little red hen saves the day.

Tompert, Ann. *Grandfather Tang's Story*. Robert Andrew Parker, illustrator. Crown, 1990. A Chinese grandfather tells his granddaughter a story using tangrams.

Walsh, Ellen Stoll. *You Silly Goose*. Harcourt Brace Jovanovich, 1992. A goose mistakes a mouse for a fox.

Wood, Audrey. *Quick as a Cricket*. Don Wood, illustrator. Child's Play (International), 1982. A boy compares himself to various animals.

# Tangram Fox

Enlarge and reproduce tangram and fox patterns.
Activity from *Grandfather Tang's Story* on page 7.

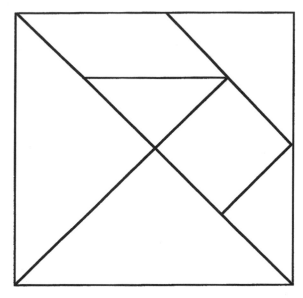

**tangram pattern**

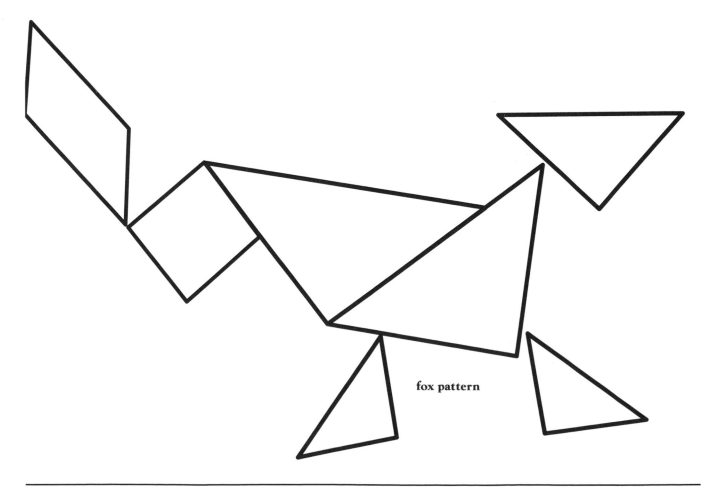

**fox pattern**

# 2
# Animal Fair

I went to the an - i - mal fair, _____ The

birds and the beasts were there, _____ The big ba-boon by the

light of the moon was comb-ing his au - burn hair. _____ The

mon - key paint-ed his toes, _____ And sat on the el - e-phant's

nose, _____ The el - e - phant sneezed, And fell on his knees, And

what be - came of the monk, the monk, the monk, the monk?

**Original Lyrics**
I went to the animal fair, The birds and the beasts were there,
The big baboon by the light of the moon, Was combing his auburn hair.
The monkey, he got drunk, And sat on the elephant's trunk.
The elephant sneezed, And fell on his knees,
And what became of the monk, the monk, the monk, the monk?

# Programming Ideas

**Themes:** animals; fairs; zoos

See Also: *Oh, Dear, What Can the Matter Be* (p.71)

## Setting the Scene

Decorate a section of the room with bright strands of twisted crepe paper or die cut different colored letters spelling out: <u>ANIMAL FAIR</u>. Have your children bring in stuffed animals for the fair and wear a colorful or striped jacket. Pass out award ribbons (*examples:* Best Stripes—tiger; Longest Ears—rabbit) for all the animals.

## Song ♫ *Animal Fair*

Ask: "Have you ever been to a fair? Ever wonder what you would see there?" Introduce the song by singing it first and acting out the lyrics. Sing and parade around the room with the stuffed animals.

## Story ▌ *A Zoo for Mister Muster*

Ask: "What zoo pet would you choose to have come home with you? Where would you keep it? What would you feed it? What games would you play?" Have children draw two pictures: their zoo pets in their homes and the homes the children make for them.

## Activities ✎

### Cooking

Read *The Best Little Monkeys in the World.* Then create your own mischief-making Monkey Shakes.

> **Monkey Shake**
> - ½ gal. milk or juice
> - 8 frozen or cold bananas (To freeze bananas: peel, cut into thirds and wrap in plastic wrap.)
> - honey to taste
> Combine in blender. Serves 16.

### Reading/Movement

Read *Jump!* or *What Would You Do if You Lived at the Zoo?* Children can imitate the sounds and movements along with the reading.

### Research/Writing

Have children research an animal and write a poem about what they learned. They can also illustrate their work.

### Craft

Make Animal Mobiles or Animal Hats.

> **Animal Mobile** (patterns on p. 11)
> 1. Photocopy and enlarge (150%) two of each animal. Cut and color the front side of both copies. Tails can be added with yarn or pipe cleaners.
>
> *Easy Version: Cut one shape for each animal (use poster board or heavier paper) and color both sides. Continue with step 3.*
>
> 2. Placing back sides together, staple or glue edges together, leaving an opening at the top to stuff with paper or polyfill.
>
> 3. Assemble mobile using coat hangers (spray painted a bright color) and fishline or yarn.
>
> This could be a group project where each child creates only <u>one</u> animal for the mobiles.

> **Animal Hats** (patterns and directions on p. 12)
>
> Have the children make animal hats using the patterns on page 12, or let them design their own animal hats.

## Books

Bennett, Jill. *The Animal Fair: Animal Verses.* Susie Jenkins-Pearce, illustrator. Viking, 1990. Animal poetry.

Carlstrom, Nancy White. *What Would You Do if You Lived at the Zoo?* Lizi Boyd, illustrator. Little, Brown, 1994. The reader explores the sounds and movement of animals.

Du Quette, Keith. *Hotel Animal.* Viking, 1994. Two lizards take a vacation at Hotel Animal that becomes more of a challenge than they had planned for.

Hall, Derek. *Baby Animals: Five Stories of Endangered Species.* John Butler, illustrator. Candlewick, 1992. Fives stories of baby: elephant, tiger, panda, polar bear, and gorilla.

Lavis, Steve. *Jump!* Dutton, 1997. A little boy, his teddy and frog interact with animals. Action book.

Lobel, Arnold. *A Zoo for Mister Muster.* HarperCollins, 1962. The zoo animals escape one night to visit their best friend, Mr. Muster.

Paxton, Tom. *Going to the Zoo.* Karen Lee Schmidt, illustrator. Morrow, 1996. Follow a family on their day at the zoo.

Standiford, Natalie. *The Best Little Monkeys in the World.* Hilary Knight, illustrator. Random House, 1987. When the parents of two little monkeys go to a party, the youngsters make mischief.

monkey

elephant

giraffe

zebra

tiger

lion

hippopotamus

panda

# Animal Hats

## Instructions

*Materials:* construction paper, crayons or markers, glue or tape, and scissors

### Directions

1. Cut a 2" strip of construction paper to fit each child's head, leaving a ½" overlap. Tape or glue to form headband.

2. Reproduce animal heads at 150% on construction paper. Color and cut out.

3. Cut slits on left and right sides in the front of the headband. Slide animal heads into slits.

4. Secure animal heads with tape or glue.

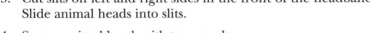

insert animal heads into slits

**sample hat**

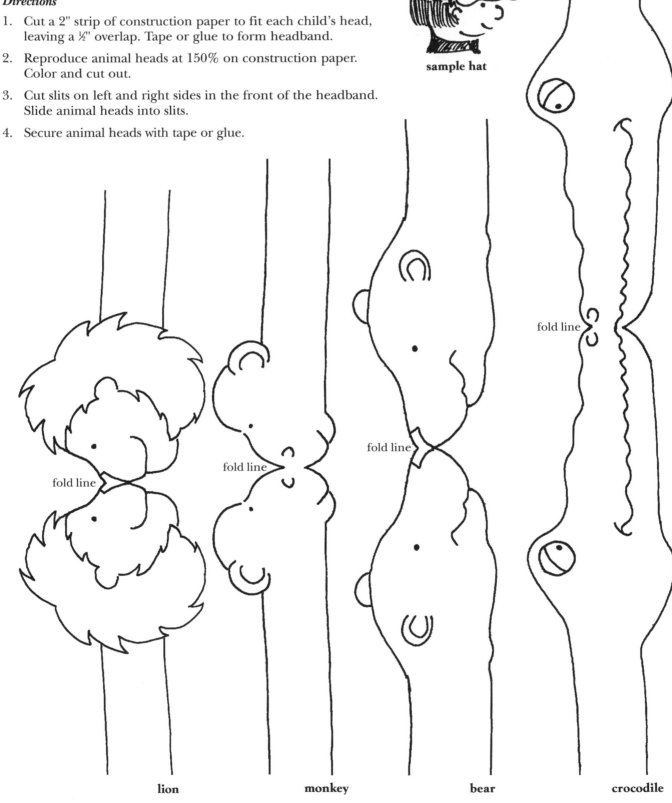

fold line

fold line

fold line

fold line

**lion**          **monkey**          **bear**          **crocodile**

# 3
# Baa, Baa, Black Sheep

Baa, baa, black sheep have you an-y wool?

"Yes, sir, yes, sir, three bags full.

One for the mas - ter and one for my dame, and

one for the lit - tle boy who lives down the lane;"

Baa, baa, black sheep have you an - y wool?

"Yes, sir, yes, sir, three bags full.

# Programming Ideas

**Themes:** sheep; wool

## Setting the Scene

Put some real wool or a wool scarf in a bag. Ask the children to reach in, describe it, and try to guess what it is. Discuss wool and where it comes from.

## Song ♫ *Baa, Baa, Black Sheep*

Ask: "Who can name this tune?" Hum the song. Ask for a volunteer to say the words or sing them. Then sing the song several times and ask the children to join in.

## Story 📖 *When Sheep Cannot Sleep*

After reading the story, have children create their own counting books using the lambs below.

## Activities ✏️

### Bulletin Board

Enlarge the picture of the lambs below to fit your bulletin board. Read *The Lamb and the Butterfly*. Each child can create a butterfly to put on the board. Enlarge and use the butterfly on page 36 or have children create their own.

### Game

Play Hide and Seek after reading *Emma's Lamb*.

### Worksheet

Find the Lamb's Lost Coat (p. 15)

## Reading/Sequencing

Read *Charlie Needs a Cloak*. Write the words "spin," "sew," "shear," "card," "cloak," and "weave" on the board. Ask: "Using the words on the board, what is the correct sequence for making a cloak?" Compare the children's answers with the last page of the book.

## Books

Alda, Arlene. *Sheep, Sheep, Sheep, Help Me Fall Asleep.* Doubleday Book for Young Readers, 1992. A child tries to fall asleep.

dePaola, Tomie. *Charlie Needs a Cloak.* Simon & Schuster Books for Young Readers, 1973. A shepherd makes a red cloak using his sheep's wool.

Fowler, Allan. *Woolly Sheep and Hungry Goats.* Rookie Read About Science series. Children's Press, 1993. Simple information about sheep and goats.

Kitamura, Satoshi. *When Sheep Cannot Sleep—The Counting Book.* Farrar, Straus & Giroux, 1986. Woolly the sheep cannot sleep.

Lewis, Kim. *Emma's Lamb.* Candlewick Press, 1991. Emma takes care of a little lost lamb.

Schal, Hannelore, and Sabine Lohf. *Making Things with Yarn.* Childrens Press, 1990. Games and crafts with yarn for children.

Shaw, Nancy. *Sheep Take a Hike.* Margot Apple, illustrator. Houghton Mifflin, 1994. Sheep are lost until they discover a trail of wool from their coats.

Sundgaard, Arnold. *The Lamb and the Butterfly.* Eric Carle, illustrator. Scholastic, 1988. A lamb converses with a butterfly.

# The Lamb's Lost Coat

Can you help this little lamb find her lost coat? Trace the string of wool to the coat.

# 4
# The Barnyard Song

**Verse 1**

I had a bird and the bird pleased me, I

fed my bird by yon-der tree; bird goes fid-dle-ee - fee.

**Verse 2**

I had a hen and the hen pleased me, I fed my hen by yon-der tree; hen goes chim-my chuck, chim-my chuck, bird goes fid-dle-ee - fee.

3. Duck: quack, quack
4. Goose: swishy, swashy
5. Sheep: baa, baa
6. Pig: griffy, gruffy
7. Cow: moo, moo
8. Horse: neigh, neigh

## Musical directions for verses 3 through 8

These verses use the music for verse 2. When you get to the ¾ measure, each new animal and its sound are added to the refrain. When you get to verse 8 the song will go as follows: I had a horse and the horse pleased me, I fed my horse by yonder tree; horse goes neigh neigh, cow goes moo moo, pig goes griffy gruffy, sheep goes baa baa, goose goes swishy swashy, duck goes quack quack, hen goes chimmy chuck chimmy chuck, bird goes fiddle-ee-fee.

# Programming Ideas

**Theme:** farms and farmers

## Setting the Scene

Invite the children to dress up like farmers for the day or dress up as one yourself. Hold up pictures of different farm animals and ask them to tell you what kinds of sounds they make. If the pictures are laminated, write the different sounds on the pictures.

## Song ♫ *The Barnyard Song*

Make larger copies of the prompt cards provided on page 18. Discuss the animals and the sounds they make. Ask for volunteers to hold the signs for the class. When an animal is mentioned as you sing or play the song, the volunteer holds the card high in the air.

You can modify the song using any animal you want, or tailor the song to match the animals in one of the books mentioned below.

## Story 📖 *Who Took the Farmer's Hat?*

Draw pictures of the animals and their interpretations of the hat (*example:* squirrel—fat brown bird). Select an object from the classroom or something else you might find on a farm and ask how the animals would interpret this object. Have the children make drawings of their ideas.

## Activities ✏️

### Cooking

Ask the children where popcorn comes from. Read *"Not Now!" Said the Cow* and make some popcorn for a snack to share.

### Craft

Distribute prompt cards for each child to color. Encourage them to draw or create a 3-D farm scene for their animals.

### Music/Reading

Read *Piggie Pie*. This book uses a song that everyone should know. Ask: "What is the song?" ("Old MacDonald") Sing it either from memory or use the book *Old MacDonald Had a Farm*.

Another music/reading activity: Sing and play "The Farmer in the Dell." Make up new lyrics after reading a book like *The Big Sneeze.* (*example:* The farmer in the barn … Hi ho the derrio, the farmer in the barn. The farmer scares the fly, etc.)

### Reading/Writing

Read *Wake Up, Wake Up.* Using the prompt card illustrations on page 18, write a predictable story in the same style.

## Books

Brown, Ruth. *The Big Sneeze.* Lothrop, Lee & Shepard, 1985. A fly makes a farmer sneeze which disturbs the other animals in humorous sequence.

Berry, Holly (illustrator). *Old MacDonald Had a Farm.* North-South Books, 1994. Illustrated version of the song with animals and musical instruments.

Lindbergh, Reeve. *The Day the Goose Got Loose.* Steven Kellogg, illustrator. Dial Books for Young Readers, 1990. A goose disrupts a farm.

Nodset, Joan L. *Who Took the Farmer's Hat?* Fritz Siebel, illustrator. HarperCollins, 1963. A farmer enlists the help of animals in finding his hat.

Oppenheim, Joanne. *"Not Now!" Said the Cow.* Chris Demarest, illustrator. Bantam Little Rooster Book, 1989. A little black crow gets no help in making popcorn.

Palatini, Margie. *Piggie Pie!* Howard Fine, illustrator. Clarion Books, 1995. A witch visits Old MacDonald's farm in search of dinner.

Wildsmith, Brian, and Rebecca Wildsmith. *Wake-Up, Wake-Up!* Harcourt, 1993. The farmer finally wakes up.

Zimmerman, Andrea, and David Clemesha. *The Cow Buzzed.* Paul Meisel, illustrator. HarperCollins Publishers, 1993. A bee sneezes and starts the confusion by passing his cold, and his buzz, to the cow. The rest of the farm animals get caught up in this mix up.

# Barnyard Song Prompt Cards

# 5
# Blue Bird

**Chorus:**

Blue bird, blue bird through the win - dow;

Blue bird, blue bird through the win - dow; Blue bird, blue bird

through the win - dow. Oh, John - ny I'm so tir - ed.

**Verse:**

Take a lit - tle girl, tap her on the shoul - der,

take a lit - tle girl, tap her on the shoul - der,

take a lit - tle girl, tap her on the shoul - der,

Oh, John - ny I'm so tir - - - ed.

# Programming Ideas

**Theme:** birds

## Setting the Scene

Ask the children to name the birds they know. List them and ask: "If you could be one of these birds, which would you choose and why?"

## Song ♫ *Blue Bird*

As the children sit at their desks, walk around the room and sing the song (chorus only, not the verse). On the line, "Oh, Johnny I'm so tired," act dramatically tired and ask a nearby child to become the next bluebird. After two or three repetitions, the children will know the song. (Encourage them to act dramatically or behave like a bird when they are the blue bird).

## Story 📖 *Bookstore Cat*

Read the book and brainstorm what might happen if a bird flew into the classroom (or library or cafeteria). Write suggestions on the board. Make up a simple story by sequencing some of the more popular suggestions. If desired, create a classroom book. Take the story and put each of the chosen suggestions on paper. Hand out a page to a student or pair of students to illustrate. Bind and keep in the reading area of the classroom or library.

## Activities ✏️

### Science/Parent Involvement

Read *Feathers for Lunch*. Distribute lists of the birds in the book. Go outside to observe birds. List or describe any that are not on the list. Homework assignment: Watch for birds with a family member and make notes on the list. Collect feathers if possible.

### Math/Measurement

Read *Inch by Inch*. Distribute inchworms (p. 21) to each student. Measure objects around the room, each other, or the bird illustrations in *Feathers for Lunch*.

### Craft

Read *Jennie's Hat*. Have children draw hats with their own personalities.

## Cooking

### Bluebird's Nest Cookies

- 2 eggs, beaten
- ½ c. sugar
- 1½ c. (12 ozs.) coconut
- fresh or frozen blueberries

Mix eggs and sugar. Add coconut and stir. Drop a large spoonful of dough onto a greased cookie sheet to form a mound. Use a smaller spoon to form the center of the nest. Bake at 350 degrees for 10 to 15 minutes or until golden. When cooled add a few bluebird eggs (blueberries) to the nest. 16 to 25 nests.

## Books

Ehlert, Lois. *Feathers for Lunch*. Harcourt Brace Jovanovich, 1990. A cat tries to catch birds in the backyard.

Johnson, Herschel. *A Visit to the Country*. Romare Bearden, illustrator. Harper & Row, 1989. A boy cares for a baby cardinal until it must return to the wild.

Keats, Ezra Jack. *Jennie's Hat*. Harper & Row, 1966. Jennie's bird friends help decorate her new hat.

Kroll, Virginia. *Wood-Hoopoe Willie*. Katherine Roundtree, illustrator. Charlesbridge, 1992. Willie wants to make music so much that his grandfather thinks a wood-hoopoe must be trapped inside him.

Lionni, Leo. *Inch by Inch*. Well-known tale of an inchworm who escapes several birds.

Ross, Michael Elsohn. *Become a Bird and Fly!* Peter Parnall, illustrator. Millbrook Press, 1992. A boy imagines himself becoming a bird.

Wheeler, Cindy. *Bookstore Cat*. Step into Reading. Step 1 Book. Random House, 1994. A cat must deal with a pigeon that comes into his bookstore.

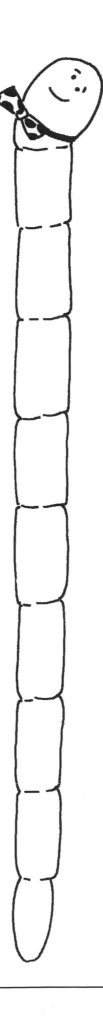

# Inch Worm

Reproduce the inch worm here, and have children use him to measure things in the room or on each other! Use with the math/measurement activity on page 20.

# 6
# Froggie Went A-Courtin'

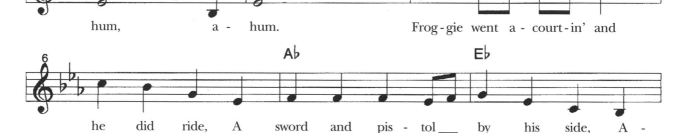

1. Frog-gie went a-court-in' and he did ride, A-hum, a-hum. Frog-gie went a-court-in' and

he did ride, A sword and pis-tol ___ by his side, A-hum, a-hum.

2. He rode up to Miss Mousie's door …
   Where he had often been before …

3. He said, "Miss Mouse, are you within?" …
   "Just lift the latch and please come in." …

4. He took Miss Mousie on his knee …
   And said, "Miss Mouse will you marry me?" …

5. "Without my Uncle Rat's consent …
   I would not marry the president." …

6. Now Uncle Rat when he came home …
   Said, "Who's been here since I've been gone?" …

7. "A very fine gentleman has been here …
   Who wishes me to be his dear." …

8. Then Uncle Rat laughed and shook his sides …
   To think his niece would be a bride …

9. Uncle Rat gave his consent …
   So they got married and off they went …

10. Where will the wedding breakfast be? …
    Away down yonder in the hollow tree …

11. What will the wedding breakfast be? …
    Two green beans and a black-eyed pea …

12. The first to come was a big white moth …
    She spread out a white tablecloth …

13. The next to come was a bumblebee …
    He danced a jig with Miss Mousie …

14. The next to come was Mister Drake …
    He ate all the wedding cake …

15. There's bread and cheese upon the shelf …
    If you want any more just sing it yourself.…

# Programming Ideas

**Theme:** frogs

## Setting the Scene

Set up an aquarium for tadpoles or a terrarium for frogs or toads. Or create a frog puppet using a green sock and button eyes and use him to introduce the song or story.

## Song ♫ *Froggie Went A-Courtin'*

Teach the children the "a-hum" pattern in the song. Sing or play the song and have the children join in on the "a-hum" parts. After the song ends, explain that the song told a story. Can the children tell you what happened in the story? Sing or play the song again, then read *Frog Went A-Courtin'* and talk about the illustrations. Explain the oral tradition of folk songs. Encourage the children to make up their own verses.

## Story 📖 *Froggy Gets Dressed*

Enlarge Froggy and his clothes on page 24 so that each fit an 8½"x 11" page. Distribute to children to cut out and color.

## Activities ✏️

### Craft

Decorate eggs (no matter the season) after reading *Bently & Egg.*

### Research

List all the facts and fictions the children know about frogs. Do the same for toads. Compare. Read a nonfiction book such as *Frogs* and review and revise the lists.

### Game

After reading *The Frog Prince*, play a Golden Ball game. Try the following or make up your own. Stand in a circle on a hard surface outside. Place a basket in the center of the circle. Each person tries to bounce a ball into the basket. (Try a tennis ball, or borrow a bigger ball from the P.E. teacher). After everyone has had a chance to throw the ball once the game begins and a person is out if he misses the basket. The last person remaining is crowned prince or princess.

### Art History

Study Monet and impressionist paintings after reading *Once Upon a Lily Pad* or share the book with the art teacher. Make a classroom impressionistic painting of a pond and lily pads. Suggestion: Use small sponge pieces and tempera or acrylic paint.

## Books

Gibbons, Gail. *Frogs*. Holiday House, 1993. A factual introduction to frogs.

Grimm, Jacob, and Wilhelm Grimm. *The Frog Prince or Iron Henry*. Binette Schroeder, illustrator. North-South Books, 1989. The traditional tale translated by Naomi Lewis.

Gwynne, Fred. *Pondlarker*. Simon & Schuster Books for Young Readers, 1990. Pondlarker, a frog, is convinced he is a prince in need of a princess's kiss.

Joyce, William. *Bently & Egg*. HarperCollins, 1992. Bently the frog is left in charge of an egg.

Langstaff, John. *Frog Went A-Courtin'*. Feodor Rojankovsky, illustrator. Harcourt Brace Jovanovich, 1955. An illustrated version of the folk song.

London, Jonathan. *Froggy Gets Dressed*. Frank Remkiewicz, illustrator. Viking, 1992. Froggy tries to get dressed for a day in the snow.

Porte, Barbara Ann. *Tale of a Tadpole*. Annie Cannon, illustrator. Orchard Books, 1997. Francine watches her tadpole change.

Sweeney, Joan. *Once Upon a Lily Pad: Froggy Love in Monet's Garden*. Kathleen Fain, illustrator. Chronicle, 1995. Two frogs patiently pose for a painter believing that he is painting their portraits.

# Froggy and His Clothes

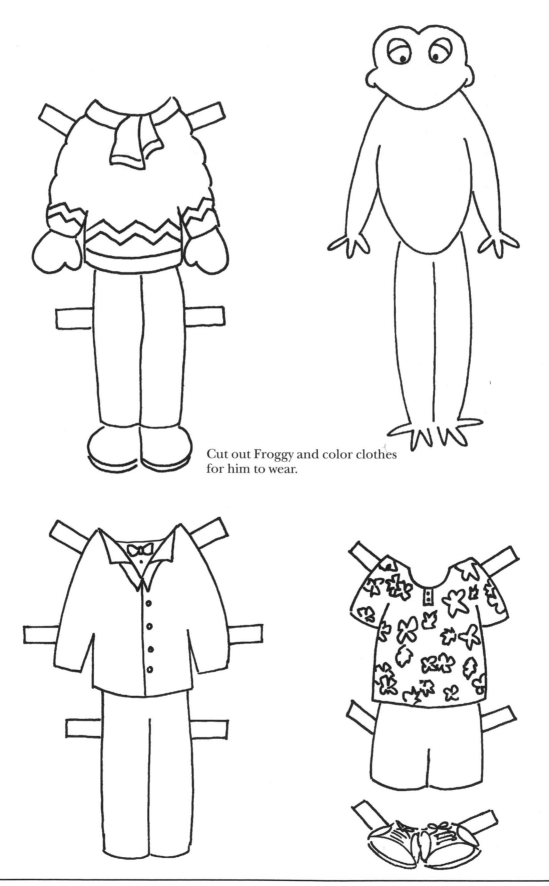

Cut out Froggy and color clothes
for him to wear.

# 7
# Hickory, Dickory, Dock

Hick - o - ry,    dick - o - ry,    dock.                    The

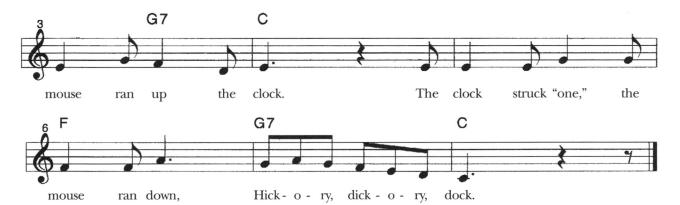

mouse    ran    up    the    clock.        The    clock    struck "one,"    the

mouse    ran down,        Hick - o - ry,    dick - o - ry,    dock.

## Additional Lyrics

Hickory, dickory, dock.
The mouse ran up the clock.
The clock struck 2,
The mouse yelled "Yahoo!"
Hickory, dickory, dock.

Hickory, dickory, dock.
The mouse ran up the clock.
The clock struck 3,
The mouse said "Look at me!"
Hickory, dickory, dock.

Hickory, dickory, dock.
The mouse ran up the clock.
The clock struck 4,
The mouse ran up once more.
Hickory, dickory, dock.

Hickory, dickory, dock.
The mouse ran up the clock.
The clock struck 5,
The mouse did a swan dive.
Hickory, dickory, dock.

Hickory, dickory, dock.
The mouse ran up the clock.
The clock struck 6,
The mouse did a few tricks.
Hickory, dickory, dock.

Hickory, dickory, dock.
The mouse ran up the clock.
The clock struck 7,
The mouse said, "I'm in heaven!"
Hickory, dickory, dock.

Hickory, dickory, dock.
The mouse ran up the clock.
The clock struck 8,
The mouse screamed,
 "This is great!"
Hickory, dickory, dock.

Hickory, dickory, dock.
The mouse ran up the clock.
The clock struck 9,
The mouse cried,
 "One more time!"
Hickory, dickory, dock.

Hickory, dickory, dock.
The mouse ran up the clock.
The clock struck 10,
Will he do it again?
Hickory, dickory, dock.

# Programming Ideas

**Themes:** clocks; telling time

## Setting the Scene

### Share the following riddles:

What has a face and hands, and says, "Tick, Tock." (clock)

What is small, has little eyes, big ears, and tells long tales? (mouse)

Tell students you are going to sing a song about a clock and a mischievous mouse.

## Song ♫ *Hickory, Dickory, Dock*

Use your own clock or make one with moveable hands. Set it for one o'clock. After singing the first verse several times, introduce some or all of the new verses. Ask for volunteers to change the time and act out the parts.

## Story 📖 *Tick Tock*

Children can make their own clock diary. Draw pictures to illustrate what happened in each hour of the day. Older children can write and illustrate.

## Activities ✏️

### Creative Writing

After singing verse ten of "Hickory, Dickory, Dock," have your students draw or write what they think the mouse will do next.

### Art

Read *Matthew's Dream*. Have children create paintings of their own dreams and invite them to share these with the group.

### Math/Telling Time

What Time Is It? worksheet (p. 27).

### Problem Solving

Where's the Cheese? worksheet (p. 28).

### Cooking

Read *The King, the Mice, and the Cheese*. Nibble on a variety of cheeses. Have the class pick a favorite and award a ribbon.

## Books

Anderson, Lena. *Tick-Tock*. Farrar, Straus & Giroux, 1998. Telling time is taught through this tale of the action-filled day of a group of animals.

Brown, Ruth. *A Dark, Dark Tale*. Dial, 1981. A mysterious and dark journey through the woods, into a castle and down the halls to a little box and its inhabitant.

Dunbar, Joyce. *Ten Little Mice*. Maria Majeivska, illustrator. Harcourt, 1990. Ten mice leave, one by one, to return to their cozy nests.

Fisher, Aileen Lucia. *The House of a Mouse: Poems*. Joan Sandin, illustrator. Harper & Row, 1988. A collection of poems on mice.

Gurney, Nancy, and Eric Gurney. *The King, the Mice, and the Cheese*. Random, 1989. The King is concerned about mice eating his cheese.

Lionni, Leo. *Matthew's Dream*. Knopf, 1991. A mouse uses his imagination to decorate his home.

Mayer, Gina. *Rosie's Mouse*. Western, 1992. Rosie, the hippo, tries to politely get rid of her uninvited guest.

Muller, Robin. *Hickory, Dickory, Dock*. Suzanne Duranceau, illustrator. Scholastic, 1994. A cat gives a party and unexpected guests show up hourly creating chaos. Lively illustrations and rhymes.

# What Time Is It?

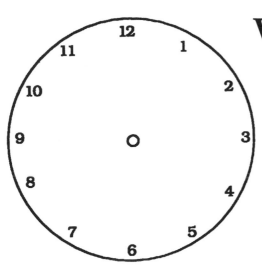

# 3 o'clock

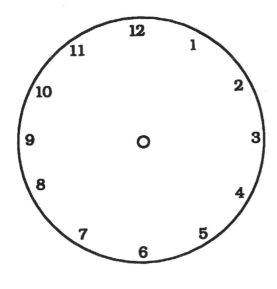

# 6 o'clock

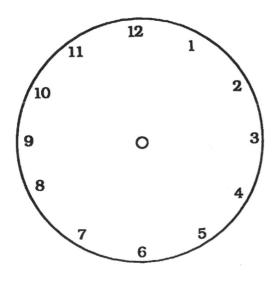

# 12 o'clock

# Where's the Cheese?

Start

CHEESE

Finish

Help the mouse find his way through the maze to the cheese.

# 8
# Little Miss Muffet

Lit - tle Miss Muf - fet Sat on a tuf - fet,

Eat - ing her curds_____ and whey;_____ There came a big spi - der, Who

sat down be - side her And fright - ened Miss Muf - fet a - way._____

## Additional Lyrics

Eating her frosted flakes…
There came a big spider who sat down beside her and said,
"Oh my goodness sakes!"

Eating her tuna fish…
There came a big spider who sat down beside her and said,
"Aren't you a sweet dish!"

Eating her peanut butter…
There came a big spider who sat down beside her and said,
"Can you spare another?"

# Programming Ideas

**Theme:** spiders

## Setting the Scene

Design a bulletin board featuring spiders. Bring a spider in a jar or make a terrarium where the spider can build a web. Observe the spider with your students.

## Song ♫ *Little Miss Muffet*

Ask: "How many of you are afraid of spiders?" Talk about some of the reasons people are afraid of spiders. Tell children that this is a song about a little girl who is also afraid of spiders. Sing or play it several times. Ask: "How many of you think you can sing it, too?" Sing it a few more times.

## Story 📖 *Be Nice to Spiders*

Talk about how the spider helped the zoo animals. Discuss other ways spiders help us. Then have children make their own spider webs using the instructions below. Alternate reading selection: *The Very Busy Spider.*

### Easy Webs

Use black construction paper, silver or white glitter, and glue. Draw a web using glue. Carefully sprinkle the glitter over the web and shake the extra glitter into a pan.

### Advanced Webs

Use wax paper and glue. Draw your web on the wax paper, carefully making lines approximately ⅛"–¼" in width. Let dry and peal. Display the webs on windows around the room.

## Activities ✏

### Craft

#### Spider Hats

1. Use black construction paper. Cut (9) 1" x 18" strips for a headband and spider legs. Accordion fold the legs.

2. Cut a circle (approx. 3" in diameter) for a head. Use white or red hole punch dots for eyes.

3. Staple legs to the headband. Then staple headband to fit.

### Craft/Science

Read *Spiders*. As a group make one or several papermache spiders. Discuss spiders: their structure, habitat, and behavior.

### Papermache Spiders

1. Use a balloon for the body.

2. Tear strips of newspaper and place in glue solution. Apply to body and let dry overnight. After the body has dried, puncture the balloon.

3. Paint the body black. Add crepe paper or construction paper strips for the legs.

### Papermache Glue Solution

- 1 c. all purpose flour
- 1¼ c. water

Mix flour and water until you get a smooth paste. Dip strips of newspaper into paste and with your fingers, clean off the excess.

## Cooking

Curds and Whey Cooking Class. As a class make oatmeal. Add raisins, honey and cinnamon to taste. Take turns acting out the song. One child plays the part of Miss Muffet, another plays the spider.

## Music

Read *Spider on the Floor* and sing the song. Ask the children to name and sing other spider songs.

## Books

Carle, Eric. *The Very Busy Spider*. Philomel, 1984. A busy spider works at spinning her web and avoiding distractions.

Clark, Emma C. *Little Miss Muffet's Count-Along Surprise*. Doubleday, 1997. Humorous counting book.

Florian, Douglas. *Insectlopedia*. Harcourt Brace, 1998. Poems and paintings.

Gibbons, Gail. *Spiders*. Holiday, 1993. Spiders: their structure, behavior, and importance.

Graham, Margaret Bloy. *Be Nice to Spiders*. HarperCollins, 1967. A boy gives his pet spider a new home.

Kirk, David. *Miss Spider's ABC*. Scholastic, 1998. Insects from throughout the alphabet celebrate Miss Spider's birthday.

Morley, Carol. *A Spider and a Pig*. Little, Brown, 1992. A fairytale about a pig, a spider, and a princess.

Russell, Bill. *Spider on the Floor*. True Kelly, illustrator. Crown, 1993. A spider creates a web that entangles many people and animals.

# 9
# My Pony

Hop, hop, hop! Nim - ble as a

top, Where 'tis smooth and where 'tis sto - ny,

Trudge a - long my lit - tle po - ny, Hop, hop, hop, hop,

hop! Nim - ble as a top.

**Verse 2**

Whoa, whoa, whoa!
How like fun we go,
Very well my little pony,
Safe's our jaunt thro' rough and stony,
Spare, spare, spare, spare, spare!
Sure enough we're there.

# Programming Ideas

**Theme:** horses

## Setting the Scene

Ask: "How many of you have every ridden a horse or pony? Who can demonstrate a walk? A trot? A canter? A gallop? A jump?" If you want the children to participate in a movement activity, ring a bell (or come up with another signal). When they hear the bell they have to freeze so they can hear you say the movement they need to do next. Ring the bell again for them to begin the new movement.

## Song ♫ *My Pony*

Clap a steady beat and ask the children to join in. Sing or play the song two or three times as they clap. Then review the words and have everyone try to sing the song.

## Story 📖 *Fritz and the Beautiful Horses* or *Pal the Pony*

Discuss the differences between horses and ponies. Ask: "If you could ride one right now, which would you choose? Why?" Have the children make Popsicle ponies (pattern and directions on p. 33).

## Activities ✏️

### Music

The song is easily divided into four sections. Write the words on four prompt cards. Divide the class into four groups, select four volunteers to hold the prompt cards in front of the class, and ask the groups to sing their parts (and only their parts). Then have the four volunteers rotate to a different group. Try singing the song again now that the groups have a different section of the song.

### Playground

Make sand sculptures in the sandbox after reading *The Sand Horse.*

### Research

Discuss horses and how they have helped mankind. Create a collage with drawings and magazine pictures of horses doing different tasks. If available, read *Snowy* to learn about an unusual job for a horse.

### Drawing

After reading *Cowardly Clyde*, ask the children to draw other monsters for Clyde to confront.

## Books

Brett, Jan. *Fritz and the Beautiful Horses.* Houghton Mifflin, 1981. Fritz the pony rescues some children.

Cole, Joanna. *Riding Silver Star.* Margaret Miller, photographer. Morrow Junior Books, 1996. Abby and her horse prepare for horse shows and enjoy a trail ride.

Doherty, Berlie. *Snowy.* Keith Bowen, illustrator. Dial Books for Young Readers, 1993. Rachel is disappointed when she cannot bring the family horse to school because he has to pull the barge.

Herman, R.A. *Pal the Pony.* Betina Ogden, illustrator. Grosset & Dunlap, 1996. Pal the pony becomes a star in his own way.

Osborne, Mary Pope. *Moonhorse.* S.M. Saelig, illustrator. Dragonfly Books, 1991. A young girl rides a winged moonhorse one night.

Peet, Bill. *Cowardly Clyde.* Houghton Mifflin, 1981. Clyde the warhorse discovers he can be brave even when frightened.

Turnbull, Ann. *The Sand Horse.* Atheneum, 1989. Michael Foreman, illustrator. A sand horse joins the white horses (froth) in the waves.

# Popsicle Pony

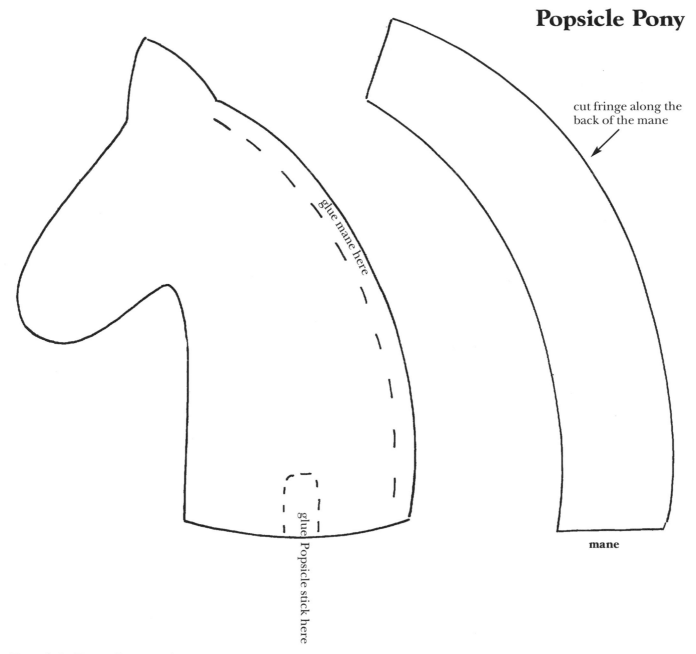

cut fringe along the
back of the mane

glue mane here

glue Popsicle stick here

mane

## Popsicle Pony Instructions

*Materials:* construction paper, small buttons, Popsicle sticks, glue or stapler, and scissors

*Directions*

1. Make tracing patterns from poster board of the pony and mane.

2. Have children trace the pony on construction paper (cut 2). Select a different color for the mane (cut 1).

3. Assemble by placing mane on one pony head and gluing in place.

4. Glue the Popsicle stick in place with one end of the stick over the dotted lines at the base of the pony's head.

5. Place a line of glue all around the edge of the one pony. Then carefully glue the mane along the back of the pony's head. Add more glue along the edge of the mane and add the second pony head. Let dry.

6. Cut a fringe along the back of the horses head to complete the mane. Glue on button eyes.

# 10
# Shoo, Fly, Don't Bother Me

# Programming Ideas

**Theme:** insects

## Setting the Scene

Pantomime shooing a bug away from you. Can the children guess what you are doing? As a class, make a chart of Bugs You Don't Shoo (*examples:* butterflies, ladybugs, dragonflies, fireflies) and Bugs You Do Shoo (*examples:* wasps, gnats, mosquitoes, flies).

## Song ♫ *Shoo, Fly, Don't Bother Me*

Stand in a circle. Sing the chorus ("Shoo, fly, don't bother me…") while pretending to shoo flies away. During the verse ("I feel … morning star") everyone joins hands and swings their arms up together while moving to the center of the circle, where their hands meet high in the air.

## Story 📖 *The Best Bug Parade*

Each child can make their own bug using paper rolls, construction paper, pom poms, pipe cleaners, or anything else handy. Have a Bug Parade and give out ribbons for the Longest, Shortest, Biggest, Smallest, etc.

## Activities ✏️

### Cooking

Read *Fresh Cider and Pie.* Serve cider and Shoo Fly Pie.

**Shoo Fly Pie**

- pie crust (any type, pre-made)
- instant pudding (1 pkg. of any flavor for each pie)
- Cool Whip or whipped cream
- raisins or currants

Make the pudding and add it to the pie crust. Cover with whipped topping. Sprinkle flies (raisins or currants) on top.

### Science

Read *Fly* by Barrie Watts. Using information drawn from the book, have students draw the two stages of a fly. Compare these to butterflies.

### Creative Writing

Read *There Was an Old Lady Who Swallowed a Fly* and *I Know an Old Lady Who Swallowed a Pie.* As a class, in pairs, or individually, make up your own versions.

### Poetry

Read *Bugs!* Hand out one bug picture (enlarged) from pages 36 and 37 for each student to color. Have the children write a poem featuring their bug.

## Books

Aylesworth, Jim. *Old Black Fly.* Stephen Gammell, illustrator. Holt, 1992. Twenty-six yucky things the old black fly did in rhyme.

Brandenberg, Franz. *Fresh Cider and Pie.* Macmillan, 1973. A captured fly outwits a spider.

Cole, Joanna. *Golly Gump Swallowed a Fly.* Bari Weissman, illustrator. Parents, 1982. A prizewinning yawner swallows a fly and then tries to get rid of it.

Greenberg, David T. *Bugs!* Lynn Munsinger, illustrator. Little, Brown, 1997. Insects are introduced in verse.

Jackson, Alison. *I Know an Old Lady Who Swallowed a Pie.* Judith Byron Schachner, illustrator. Dutton Children's Books, 1997. A new version of the traditional rhyme featuring an old lady who comes for Thanksgiving dinner.

Murphy, Stuart J. *The Best Bug Parade.* (Mathstart Series) Holly Keller, illustrator. Harper Trophy, 1972. Big and small bugs are on parade in this combination math lesson and colorful event.

Peters, Lisa Westberg. *When the Fly Flew In.* Brad Sneed, illustrator. Dial, 1994. A pesky fly causes a group of animals to clean their room.

Talback, Simms. *There Was an Old Lady Who Swallowed a Fly.* Viking, 1997. A revision of the classic nursery rhyme.

Watts, Barrie. Fly. Silver Burdett, 1997. Photos and brief text explore the life cycle of the greenbottle fly.

# Bug Poetry Pictures

**mosquito**

**butterfly**

**gnats**

**dragonfly**

**bee**

**ladybug**

fly

firefly

spider

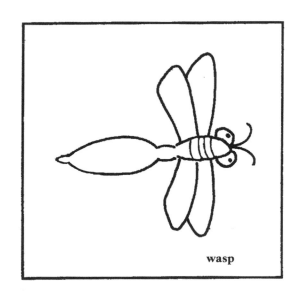

wasp

grasshopper

ant

# 11
# Three Little Kittens

1. Three lit - tle kit - tens, they lost their mit - tens, And
they be - gan to cry. _____ "Oh, Moth - er dear, we
sad - ly fear Our mit - tens we have lost." _____ "What?
Lost your mit-tens you naught - y kit-tens! Then you shall have no pie."
"Me - ow, me - ow, me - ow, meow!
"Me - ow, me - ow, me - ow, meow!"

2. Three little kittens,
    they found their mittens,
And they began to cry,
"Oh, Mother dear, see here, see here,
Our mittens we have found."
"What? Found your mittens?
You lovely kittens,
Then you shall have some pie."
"Meow, meow, meow, meow.
Meow, meow, meow,meow."

3. Three little kittens,
     put on their mittens,
And soon ate up the pie;
"Oh, Mother dear, we greatly fear,
Our mittens we have soiled."
"What? Soiled your mittens?
You naughty kittens!"
Then they began to sigh.
"Meow, meow, meow, meow.
Meow, meow, meow, meow."

4. Three little kittens,
    they washed their mittens,
And hung them out to dry,
"Oh, Mother dear, see here, see here,
Our mittens we have washed."
"What? Washed your mittens?
You lovely kittens,
But I smell a rat close by."
"Meow, meow, meow, meow.
Meow, meow, meow, meow."

# Programming Ideas

**Themes:** cats; weather

## Setting the Scene

Transform your storytime area into a Cat Nap Corner. Throw some soft pillows or blankets in a corner with pictures of cats decorating the walls and books about cats displayed.

## Song ♫ *Three Little Kittens*

Sing or say the "meow" section of the song and have the children imitate you. After rehearsing the "meows" a few times, sing or play a recording of the song and gesture to the children to join in each time the "meow" section starts.

## Story 📖 *Duncan & Dolores*

Enlarge and distribute pictures of the cat on this page. Design outfits for the cat to wear.

## Activities ✏️

### Research

Read *Have You Seen My Cat?* Discuss the different kinds of cats and their environments. Research the habitats of the wild cats.

### Game

Play the Missing Mitten Game. Using the mitten pattern on page 40, make ten to twelve pairs of mittens out of multi-colored sheets of paper or wallpaper samples. Laminate. Remove one mitten and place the rest in a bag or box. Mix well and have students match pairs to discover which is missing a mitten.

### Sequencing

Enlarge a copy of the verse illustrations on page 40 for each child. The children can color, cut, sequence, and glue to another sheet.

### Creative Writing

Read *Caps, Hats, Socks & Mittens.* Compare climates, clothing and activities during different seasons. Make up new verses for the different seasons or bring in a variety of seasonal clothing to try on for fun.

## Books

Arnold, Katya. *Meow!* Vladimir Suteev, illustrator. Holiday House, 1998. A dog discovers the sounds different animals make.

Boivin, Kelly. *Where Is Mittens?* Clovis Martin, illustrator. Childrens Press, 1990. A child's lost cat turns up accompanied by four new kittens.

Borden, Louise. *Caps, Hats, Socks & Mittens: A Book about the Four Seasons.* Lillian Hoban, illustrator. Scholastic, 1989. Simple text and illustrations describe some of the pleasures of each season.

Brett, Jan. *The Mitten: A Ukrainian Folktale.* Putnam, 1989. Several animals sleep snugly in Nicki's lost mitten until the bear sneezes.

Carle, Eric. *Have You Seen My Cat?* Simon & Schuster Books for Young Readers, 1987. A young boy sees many kinds of cats as he searches for his own.

Preston, Edna. *Where Did My Mother Go?* Chris Conover, illustrator. Four Winds, 1978. Little cat searches everywhere for his mother convinced that she is lost.

Samuels, Barbara. *Duncan & Dolores.* Bradbury, 1989. Dolores learns to curb her smothering ways and wins the affection of her new pet, Duncan.

# Missing Mitten Game / Sequencing Cards

**Missing Mitten Game**

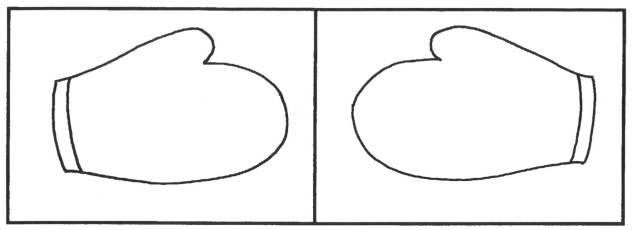

Make ten to twelve pairs of unique pairs mittens for the Missing Mitten Game.

**Sequencing Cards**

Make a copy of these four illustrations from the "Three Little Kittens" for each child to color and sequence.

# 12
# Where Has My Little Dog Gone?

Oh where, oh where has my lit - tle dog gone? Oh where, oh where can he be? _____ With his tail cut short and his ears cut long, oh where, oh where can he be? _____

## Additional Lyrics

Oh where, oh where has my little dog gone?
Oh where, oh where can he be?
Is he under a tree, hiding from me?
Oh where, oh where can he be?

Oh where, oh where has my little dog gone?
Oh where, oh where can he be?
Is he in the barn, away from harm?
Oh where, oh where can he be?

Oh where, oh where has my little dog gone?
Oh where, oh where can he be?
Is he behind the bed, asleep on his head?
Oh where, oh where can he be?

Oh where, oh where has my little dog gone?
Oh where, oh where can he be?
Is he under the rug, snug as a bug?
Oh where, oh where can he be?

# Programming Ideas

**Theme:** dogs

## Setting the Scene

Make a "Lost Pet" poster like the one below, and read it to the class. Ask your students if they have ever lost a pet. What did they do to find it? How would they describe their pets if they were lost? Individually or as a group, design a "Lost Pet" poster.

## Song ♫ *Where Has My Little Dog Gone?*

Explain that the song is about someone looking for a dog. After singing the song, ask the children to describe the dog (little, short tail, long ears). Could this be the same dog that is in the poster? Compare the description in the song with the poster.

## Story 📖 *The Adventures of Taxi Dog*

Talk about the different things Maxi saw riding in a car. Compare the type of life Maxi had to that of a dog that lives on a farm or in the country. Write and illustrate an adventure for Maxi.

## Activities ✏️

### Music

Enlarge and cut out the dog and four drawings (p. 43). Color them all and mount them on poster board. Using self-adhesive Velcro, put one piece on the back of each of the drawings and another piece to the back of the dog. You can then stick him to the back of one of the drawings. Sing the additional verses using the cards and have children guess where the dog is hidden.

### Game

Animal Rescue! Bring in a stuffed animal. When the class is out of the room, hide it. Have the children hunt for the "lost" animal. Give additional clues if necessary and a reward for the rescuer!

### Cooking

Reward your students' good behavior with these "Doggie Biscuits."

**Melt-In-Your-Mouth Dog Biscuits**

- ¾ c. margarine
- ¼ c. sugar
- 2 c. all-purpose flour

Mix all ingredients and chill at least a half hour.

On a lightly floured surface, roll dough ½" thick and cut with cookie cutter shaped like a dog biscuit. Or, roll some of the dough into a long coil, cut pieces 2 to 2½" in length. With a plastic knife, cut a slit on both ends. spread them open and press with the palm to flatten. Round the ends with your fingers to resemble dog biscuits. Bake at 350° for 10 to 15 minutes or until set. Yields 2 dozen.

### Drawing

Read *Moe the Dog in Tropical Paradise*. Ask children to paint or color pictures of their own tropical paradise.

## Books

Barracca, Debra, and Sal Barracca. *The Adventures of Taxi Dog.* Mark Buehner, illustrator. Dial, 1991. Jim, the taxi driver, adopts a homeless dog named Maxi.

Eastman, P.D. *Go, Dog, Go!* Random, 1961. The humorous and inventive antics of dogs.

Gibbons, Gail. *Dogs.* Holiday, 1996. An overview of dogs: history, breeds, and anatomy.

Hill, Eric. *Where's Spot?* Putnam, 1980. A mother dog finds other animals while searching for her lost puppy.

McNeal, Tom, and Laura McNeal. *The Dog Who Lost His Bob.* John Sandford, illustrator. Whitman, 1996. A dog escape taking a bath, but gets lost in the process.

Perkins, Al. *Digging-est Dog.* Eric Gurney, illustrator. Random, 1975. The countryside is covered with holes because Sam, the dog, must prove himself to his friends.

Stanley, Diane. *Moe the Dog in Tropical Paradise.* Elise Primavera, illustrator. Putnam, 1992. Moe creates his own tropical paradise in the dead of winter.

Zion, Gene. *Harry the Dirty Dog.* Margaret Bloy Graham, illustrator. Harper, 1956. When Harry runs away, he gets so dirty his family doesn't recognize him.

# Where Has the Little Dog Gone?

Enlarge and color these pieces for use
with the music activity on page 42.

# 13 A-Tisket, A-Tasket

A - tis - ket, a - tas - ket. A green and yel - low bas - ket, I wrote a let - ter to my love And on the way I dropped it. I dropped it, I dropped it. And on the way I dropped it, A lit - tle dog - gie picked it up and put it in his pock - et.

# Programming Ideas

**Themes:** letter writing; post office

## Setting the Scene

Reproduce the Tisket-Tasket letter below. Put it in an unsealed envelope and read it to your class.

> Dear
>
> Please help me. I wrote a letter to my friend, but on the way to the post office I dropped it. A cute little dog picked it up and put it in his pocket. Can you believe that? Anyway, I rewrote the letter. Would you be so kind as to mail it for me?
>
> Thank you.
>    Sincerely,
>
>    Your friend

## Song ♫ *A-Tisket, A-Tasket*

Ask: "Does the Tisket-Tasket letter sound familiar?" Explain that it reminds you of a song you know. Sing the song once or twice then have the children form a circle. While singing, one child carries the letter and skips around the circle. At the end of the song, he drops the letter behind another student. It is now this child's turn to carry the letter. Change the tempo for added fun.

## Story 📖 *No Mail for Mitchell*

After reading the story, have the children write a letter to themselves saying what they like about themselves. Put a real stamp on the letters and mail them.

## Activities ✏️

### Map Skills

Read *Hail to Mail*. Find the locations of the cities and countries mentioned in the book on a map. Route the mail's journey. Locate pen pals in other countries on the Internet and write to them. Possible websites to use include Intercultural E-Mail Classroom Connections (www.stolaf.edu/network/iecc) and Key Pals Global Connections (www.learningspace.org/global_conn/gcline/findpal.html)

### Craft

Let the children make their own tisket tasket baskets (patterns and instructions on page 46).

### Storytelling

Read *Elephants Aloft*. Using the book, children can retell the story in their own words using the prepositions.

### Writing

Create mailboxes for each student. (Use shoe boxes and attach flags with fasteners). Write an address on each. Place them around the room or on each desk. Write postcards to classmates using plain index cards (Write the message on one side and the address on the other. Draw a stamp). Children can deliver the mail themselves or take turns.

## Books

Ahlberg, Janet, and Allan Ahlberg. *The Jolly Postman: Or Other People's Letters*. Little, Brown, 1986. A postman delivers mail to fairy tale characters.

Appelt, Kathi. *Elephants Aloft*. Keith Baker, illustrator. Harcourt, 1993. Prepositions and illustrations tell of the travels of two young elephants and an air balloon.

Bang, Molly. *Delphine*. Morrow, 1988. Molly gets a surprise package from her grandmother.

Denslow, Sharon Phillips. *Hazel's Circle*. Sharon McGinley-Nally, illustrator. Four Winds, 1992. Hazel and her pet rooster share adventures while delivering eggs in a basket.

Leedy, Loren. *Messages in the Mailbox: How to Write a Letter*. Holiday, 1991. An alligator teaches her students how to write a letter.

Marshak, Samuel. *Hail to Mail*. Vladimir Radunsky, illustrator. Holt, 1995. A certified letter travels the world in poetry.

Siracusa, Catherine. *No Mail for Mitchell*. Random, 1990. A dog postman named Mitchell never gets letters.

# Tisket-Tasket Basket

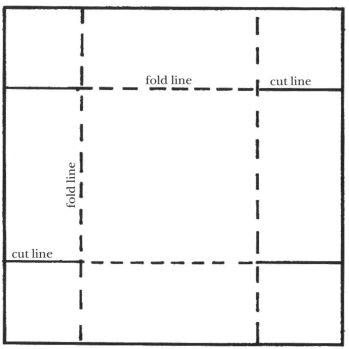

fold line

cut line

fold line

cut line

**basket** Cut on the solid cut lines, and fold on the dotted lines.

**handle**

### Tisket-Tasket Basket Instructions

*Simple Version: construction paper, glue*

1. For each basket: Cut (1) 8"x 8" square and (1) 10"x 1" strip.

2. Draw a 2" border on each side and mark for cut or fold lines as shown above.

3. Cut on cut lines and fold on fold lines.

4. Paste or staple sides together to finish the basket.

5. Add handle to basket.

*Advanced Version: plastic tubs, yarn, glue*

1. For each basket: Use a butter or yogurt tub.

2. Turn tub upside down on a work table.

3. Place glue on the bottom half of the basket.

4. Wrap thick yarn around the tub making sure the entire surface is covered.

5. Repeat process until tub is covered. Dry.

6. Add a handle made out of construction paper.

# 14
# Diddle, Diddle Dumpling

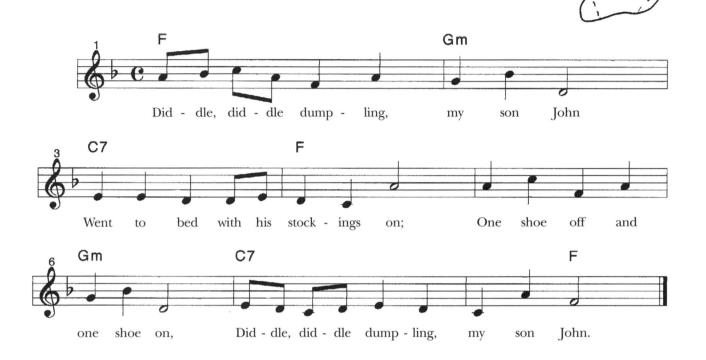

Did - dle, did - dle dump - ling, my son John
Went to bed with his stock - ings on; One shoe off and
one shoe on, Did - dle, did - dle dump - ling, my son John.

# Programming Ideas

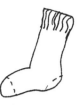

**Themes:** clothing; shoes and socks

## Setting the Scene

Bring in several pairs of socks or several pairs of shoes. Put them in a bag or box. With the children seated in front of you, draw from the bag and put one sock (or shoe) on. Then draw another sock. Ask: "Do the socks match? Do they make a pair?" Continue trying on socks until you find a match.

## Song ♫ *Diddle Diddle Dumpling*

Recite the entire nursery rhyme. Then go through the rhyme one line at a time and have the children repeat after you. Sing the song. Repeat the song and have the children sing each line after you. Make up movements or try the Diddle, Diddle Dumpling Game.

Game Directions: Ask for a volunteer to come up. He or she can either give you one of his shoes or you can provide one. Ask the volunteer to leave the room or cover their eyes. The children sing as you walk about and hand the shoe to someone. At the end of the song, everyone puts their hands behind their backs pretending to have the shoe. The volunteer gets three guesses as to who has the shoe. If he guesses correctly, then he gets to choose the next person to go out of the room. If he guess incorrectly, the person with the shoe goes out of the room.

## Story 📖 *Shoes, Shoes, Shoes*

Bring in a variety of shoes (*examples:* galoshes, bowling shoes, swim fins) to try on and play with. Talk about the different types of shoes and their uses. Then read *Shoes, Shoes, Shoes* for a world tour about the things people wear on their feet.

## Activities ✏️

### Cooking

Read *Dumpling Soup* and then enjoy some dumplings.

#### Oriental Dumplings

* 5 c. soup broth (chicken, beef, or vegetable)

Dumpling Dough
* 1 c. flour
* ½ tsp. salt
* 2 Tbs. milk
* 4 Tbs. oil
* 2 small eggs

Mix flour and salt in a bowl. Add milk, oil, and eggs. Knead dough until smooth. With thumb and forefinger pinch dough off (about the size of a quarter) and drop in simmering broth. Cook about 10 min. Take out and serve warm.

#### Traditional Dumplings

Follow the Oriental recipe, but instead of pinching dough, roll out about ⅛ of it on a floured surface (cover rest of dough with a cloth) until paper thin. Cut into 3" squares. Place 1 tsp. of filling in center (rectangular shape), fold dough over from one side, then roll over until it meets the other side. Press ends of roll to seal. Simmer in broth approximately 20 minutes. Take out and serve warm.

*Filling (make ahead)*
* 1 pkg. frozen chopped spinach or broccoli thawed and drained
* 8 oz. ground turkey cooked
* 1 Tb. soy sauce

### Game

Match the Sock Game. Cut out twenty sock shapes (ten pairs) using the pattern on page 50. Have children color one side, and then laminate. Play a matching game.

### Bulletin Board

Decorate a bulletin board with pictures and drawings (pp. 49-50) of shoes. Select action words to describe the different things the shoes do (stomp, clop, jump, tap) and add those to the bulletin board.

### Creative Writing

After reading *Shoes, Shoes, Shoes.* Ask: "What is your favorite kind of shoe? What do you do in those shoes?" Ask the children to write a story about their favorite shoes.

## Books

Hughes, Shirley. *Two Shoes, New Shoes.* Lothrop, 1986. Rhyming book about clothes.

McMillan, Bruce. *One, Two, One Pair!* Scholastic, 1996. Concept book about pairs.

Morris, Ann. *Shoes, Shoes, Shoes.* Lothrop, 1995. Thirty-one shoes from other cultures are featured.

Oppenheim, Joanne. *Left and Right.* Rosanne Litzinger, illustrator. Harcourt, 1989. Two brothers, who are shoemakers, learn to rely on each others' strengths.

Rattigan, Jama Kim. *Dumpling Soup.* Lillian Hsu-Flanders, illustrator. Little, Brown, 1993. Marisa tries to make dumplings.

Seuss, Dr. *The Foot Book.* Random House, 1968. Feet, feet and more feet in Seuss's inimitable style.

Winthrop, Elizabeth. *Shoes.* William Joyce, illustrator. HarperCollins, 1986. Rhyming verse about shoes and feet.

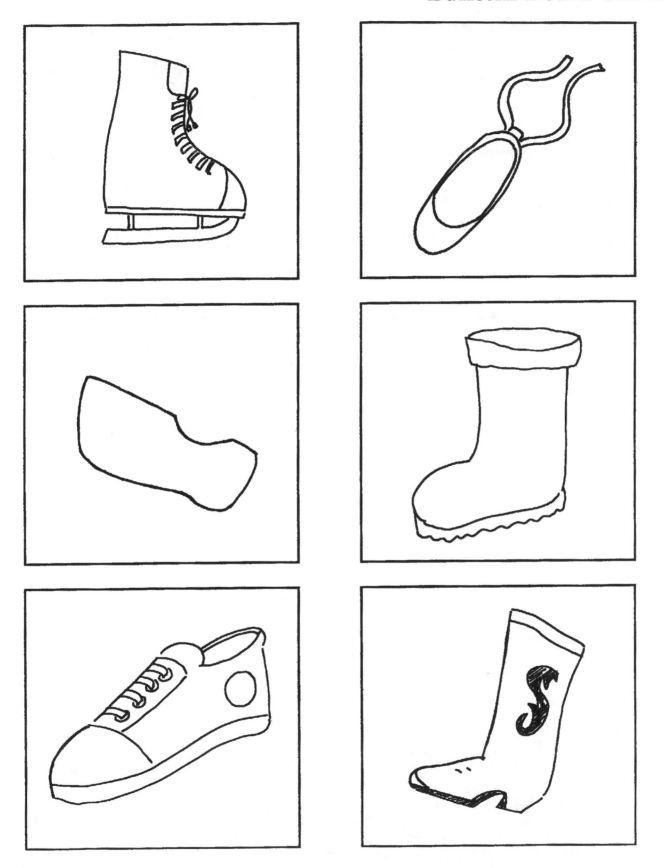

# Bulletin Board Shoes / Match the Sock Game

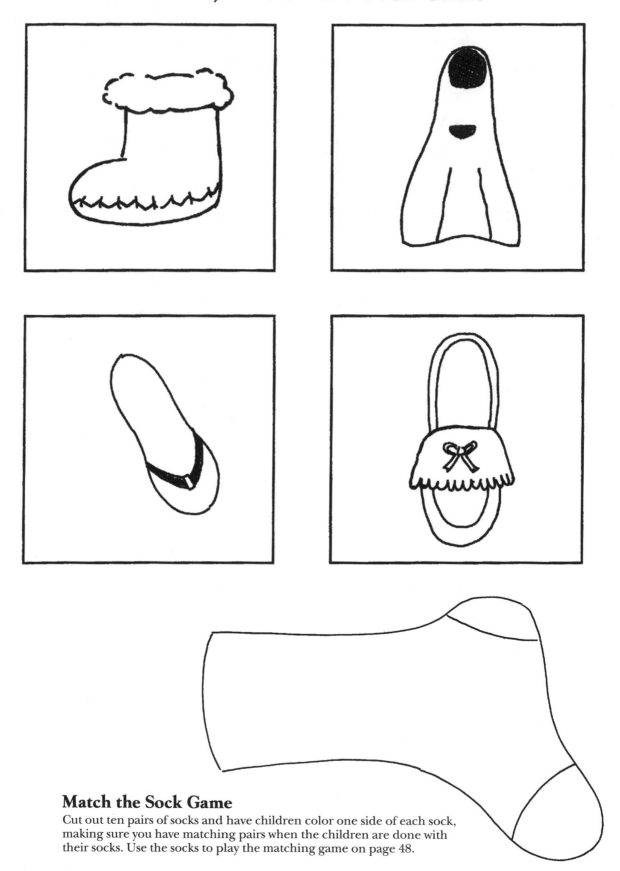

## Match the Sock Game
Cut out ten pairs of socks and have children color one side of each sock, making sure you have matching pairs when the children are done with their socks. Use the socks to play the matching game on page 48.

# 15
# Fiddle-Dee-Dee

Fid - dle - dee dee,   Fid - dle - dee - dee,   The   fly   has mar - ried the

bum - ble bee.   (1.) Says the fly,   says he, "Will you mar - ry   me   and

live   with me,   sweet bum - ble bee?"   Fid - dle - dee - dee,

Fid - dle - dee - dee,   The   fly   has mar - ried the bum - ble bee.

2. Fiddle-dee-dee, Fiddle-dee-dee,
   The fly has married the bumblebee.
   Says the bee, says she, "I'll live under your wing,
   And you shan't ever feel my sting."
   Fiddle-dee-dee, etc.

3. Fiddle-dee-dee, Fiddle-dee-dee,
   The fly has married the bumblebee.
   When the two were wed they went out to fly,
   They sailed away across the sky.
   Fiddle-dee-dee, etc.

4. Fiddle-dee-dee, Fiddle-dee-dee,
   The fly has married the bumblebee.
   All the bees did buzz and the flies did sing,
   And bluebells one and all did ring.
   Fiddle-dee-dee, etc.

5. Fiddle-dee-dee, Fiddle-dee-dee,
   The fly has married the bumblebee.
   Then the bumblebee did wink her eye
   To think that she had caught the fly.
   Fiddle-dee-dee, etc.

# Programming Ideas

**Themes:** insects; Valentines Day

## Setting the Scene

Ask: "Have you ever been in love? Have you ever been married? Have you ever been to a wedding? Have you ever seen two bugs get married?"

## Song ♫ *Fiddle-Dee-Dee*

This is a song about two insects that love each other very much and decide to get married. After you introduce the song, act it out. Give the bride a bouquet to carry and the groom a paper corsage. The rest of the class can be guests.

## Story 📖 *The Best Bug Parade*

Create your own imaginary bugs or use *Bugs, Bugs, Bugs*. Have a parade. Arrange the bugs in various orders: size, color, length, etc. Make comparisons in the classroom using superlatives. There are excellent activities suggested in the back of *Bugs, Bugs, Bugs*.

## Activities ✏️

### Art

Clay Beehive

1. Form long ropes of clay with your hands—approximately ¼" in diameter.
2. Make a circle 5" in diameter to form the base. Cut off the excess and pinch to close.
3. Add a second layer and wind the clay around to form a cone.
4. With a plastic knife cut a hole in one side.

### Reading

Read *Busy Buzzing Bumblebees and Other Tongue Twisters*. Have the children try some of the twisters.

### Creative Writing

Read *Roses Are Pink, Your Feet Stink*. Write funny valentines.

## Math/Graphing

Graph your favorite bugs. You might use the insect illustrations on pages 36 and 37 to start your bug list.

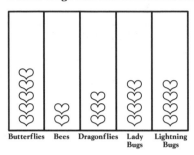

**Which Bugs Are Loved the Most?**

| Butterflies | Bees | Dragonflies | Lady Bugs | Lightning Bugs |

## Books

Better Homes and Gardens. *Bugs, Bugs, Bugs*. Meredith, 1989. Art, craft, cooking, science and nature activities.

Carle, Eric. *The Very Quiet Cricket*. Philomel, 1990. A cricket discovers other insects and a wonderful sound.

Davenier, Christine. *Leon and Albertine*. Dominic Barth, illustrator. Orchard, 1998. A pig tries hard to win the affections of a very disinterested chicken.

De Groat, Diane. *Roses Are Pink, Your Feet Really Stink*. Morrow, 1996. An animal youngster writes mean valentines to his classmates, but learns a lesson in the end.

Murphy, Stuart J. *The Best Bug Parade*. Holly Keller, illustrator. HarperCollins, 1996. The concept of size is introduced with a parade of bugs.

Ross, Kathy. *Crafts for Kids Who Are Wild about Insects*. Sharon Lane Holm, illustrator. Millbrook, 1997. Twenty simple craft projects.

Schwartz, Alvin. *Busy Buzzing Bumblebees and Other Tongue Twisters*. Paul Meisel, illustrator. HarperCollins, 1992. A collection of tongue twisters for beginning readers.

West, Colin. *"Buzz, Buzz, Buzz" Went the Bumblebee*. Candlewick, 1996. The journey of a bee and some silly animals.

# 16
# Hey Diddle Diddle

Hey did - dle did - dle, the cat and the fid - dle, The

cow jumped o - ver the moon._____ The lit - tle dog laughed _____ to

see such sport, And the dish ran a - way with the spoon._____

# Programming Ideas

**Theme:** moon

## Setting the Scene

Use a feltboard and place a large white felt circle on the board. Talk about the moon. Ask: "Is the moon always round? (Place black sections to demonstrate). Is the moon made of cheese? Is there a man on the moon? Can you jump over the moon?"

## Song ♫ *Hey Diddle Diddle*

Ask: "Does anyone know the rhyme about a cow who jumps over the moon? Can you tell it to the class? Does anyone know the song version?" Sing the song several times and then have the kids illustrate their ideas.

## Story ▤ *Moonstruck*

Introduce the story by telling the children this is the real story of how the cow jumped over the moon.

## Activities ✎

### Cooking

Bake some mooncakes.

#### Mooncake Cookies

- 1 c. margarine
- ½ c. confectioners' sugar
- 1 tsp. vanilla
- ¼ tsp. salt
- 2¼ c. all-purpose flour

Mix margarine, sugar, and vanilla thoroughly. Add flour and salt and mix until the dough holds. Shape into 1" balls. Flatten slightly with the palm of the hand, and make some crescent moon shapes as well. Bake at 400 degrees for about 8 to 10 minutes or until set, not brown. While still warm, roll in confectioner's sugar.

### Craft

Read *Cows Can't Fly* and have the students draw their own flying animals. Make a mobile.

### Movement

Use chalk and draw moons (different phases) on the concrete outside. Give everyone a chance to practice jumping over the moon. **Or** read *Moondance* and create your own moondances.

## Math/Science

Moon's Phases worksheet (p. 55) **Or** make a telescope.

### Telescope Instructions

Materials: Paper towel tubes, rubber bands, construction paper, glue, dark blue or black tissue paper or dark wrapping paper.

1. Cover the tube with construction paper.
2. Cut a circle out of tissue or wrapping paper two inches larger than the diameter of the tube end. Punch a hole in the center and secure on the end of the tube with a rubber band.

## Books

Asch, Frank. *Moondance*. Scholastic, 1993. A bear wants to dance with the moon.

Babcock, Chris. *No Moon, No Milk!* Mark Teague, illustrator. Crown, 1993. A stubborn cow refuses to give milk until she can go to the moon.

Brown, Paula. *Moon Jump: A Countdown*. Puffin, 1996. Counting book: cow contest.

Choldenko, Gennifer. *Moonstruck: The True Story of the Cow Who Jumped Over the Moon*. Paul Yalowitz, illustrator. Hyperion, 1997. A determined cow trains to jump the moon.

Fowler, Allan. *So That's How the Moon Changes Shape!* Childrens, 1991. A simple explanation of the phases of the moon.

Milgrim, David. *Cows Can't Fly*. Viking, 1998. A boy draws flying cows and sees his drawings come to life.

Shea, Pegi Deitz. *New Moon*. Cathryn Falwell, illustrator. Boyds Mills, 1996. Vinnie and his brother explore phases of the moon.

Speed, Toby. *Two Cool Cows*. Barry Root, illustrator. Putnam, 1995. Two really cool cows jump to the moon and find many others already there.

# Moon's Phases

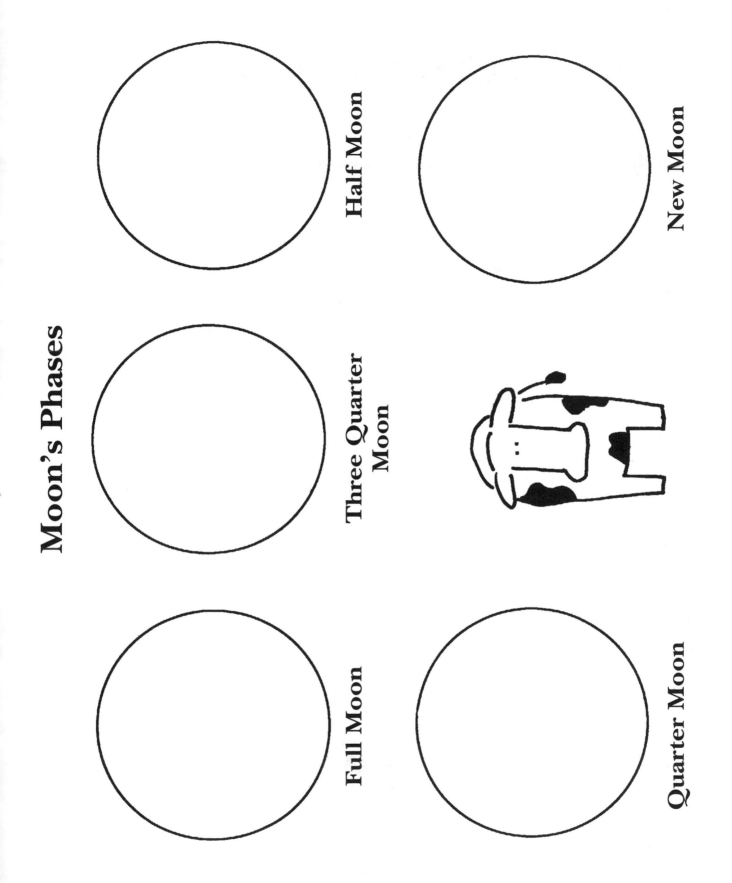

**Half Moon**

**New Moon**

**Three Quarter Moon**

**Full Moon**

**Quarter Moon**

# 17
# Humpty Dumpty

Hump - ty Dump - ty sat on a wall.
Hump ty Dump - ty had a great fall. All the king's hors - es and
all the king's men could - n't put Hump - ty Dump - ty to -
geth - er a - gain._____

# Programming Ideas

**Theme:** eggs

## Setting the Scene

Take key words from Mother Goose rhymes and see how many hints you have to give before the class guesses the rhyme. (*examples:* tuffet—Little Miss Muffet; tails, sheep, little—Little Bo-Peep; wall, fall—Humpty Dumpty.)

## Song ♫ *Humpty Dumpty*

Reproduce the picture of Humpty Dumpty on page 58 and distribute to each child. Make a transparency of the facial expressions on page 58. Have the children write the rhyme on the page or you can write the poem on the original picture before copying. Sing the song two or three times and ask them to sing along. Let them draw in faces.

## Story 📖 *Little Lumpty* or *Whatever Happened to Humpty Dumpty*

Ask someone to recite or sing Humpty Dumpty to the class. Ask: "What happens next? Any ideas?" List children's answers on the board). Read *Little Lumpty* or "Humpty Dumpty" in *Whatever Happened to Humpty Dumpty*.

Extension: Ask the class to brainstorm reasons why Humpty Dumpty fell. Read "Bedtime" from *Whatever Happened to Humpty Dumpty*. Give extra credit or a prize to anyone who writes a second verse.

## Activities ✏

### Writing

Read *Eggbert* and write postcards to him about exciting places you have been or exciting things you have done.

### Science

Share *Egg: A Photographic Story of Hatching*. Compare the similarities and differences of bird eggs to those of the tortoise, corn snake, gecko, butterfly, ladybug, dragonfly, frog, newt, fish, and slug.

### Advertising

Read *Too Many Chickens*. Have the children create their own "For Sale" signs. Post around the room.

## Art

Design a beautiful egg on paper. Read *The Most Wonderful Egg in the World*. Crown all the children as princes and princesses for having such wonderful eggs. OR ask them to draw an egg with an imaginary creature emerging. The egg can be any size and the creature can be friendly or monstrous. Read *Nessa's Story*, a tale inspired by an Inuit legend of a huge, shaggy animal called a silaq which hatches from a large white egg.

## Books

Bourgeois, Paulette. *Too Many Chickens*. Bill Slavin, illustrator. Little, Brown, 1990. A teacher and her students deal with a dozen chicks after they hatch in the classroom.

Burton, Robert. *Egg: A Photographic Story of Hatching*. Jane Burton and Kim Taylor, photographers. Dorling Kindersley, 1994. Photographic record of the hatching of several different animals.

Greenberg, David T. *Whatever Happened to Humpty Dumpty?: And Other Surprising Sequels to Mother Goose Rhymes*. S.D. Schindler, illustrator. Little, Brown, 1999. Humorous sequels to twenty rhymes.

Heine, Helme. *The Most Wonderful Egg in the World*. Athenium, 1983. The chicken that lays the most wonderful egg will become a princess.

Imai, Miko. *Little Lumpty*. Candlewick, 1994. Little Lumpty wants to sit on Humpy Dumpty's wall.

Lionni, Leo. *An Extraordinary Egg*. Alfred A. Knopf, 1994. A frog brings home what she thinks is a chicken's egg.

Luenn, Nancy. *Nessa's Story*. Neil Waldman, illustrator. Athenium, 1994. A young Inuit girl wants a story of her own to tell.

Ross, Tom. *Eggbert the Slightly Cracked Egg*. Rex Barron, illustrator. G.P. Putnam, 1994. A slightly cracked egg has to leave the refrigerator.

# Humpty Dumpty

Reproduce Humpty Dumpty for children to complete and color. Make transparencies of the expressions below to show some of Humpty Dumpty's emotions while singing the song.

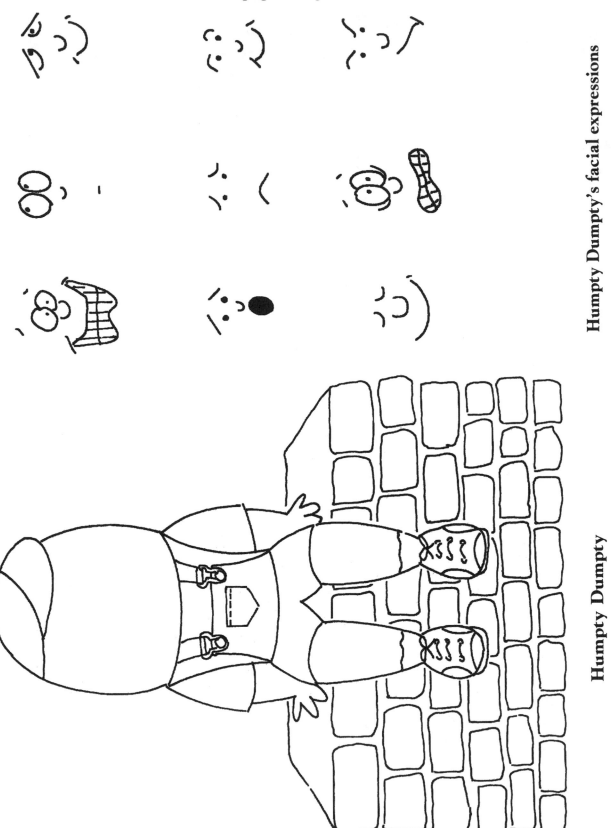

# 18
# Jack and Jill

WATER

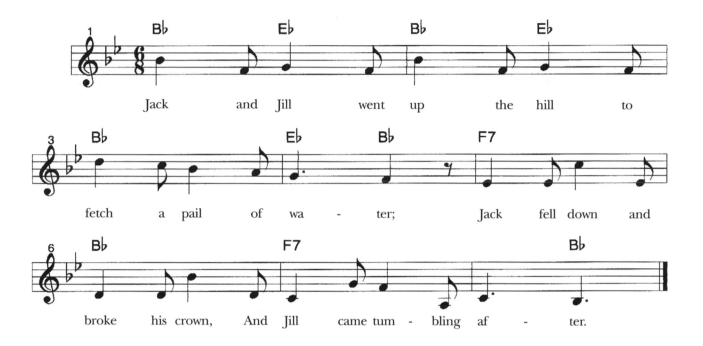

Jack and Jill went up the hill to
fetch a pail of wa - ter; Jack fell down and
broke his crown, And Jill came tum - bling af - ter.

2. Then up Jack got and off did trot,
   As fast as he could caper,
   To old Dame Dob, who patched his nob
   With vinegar and brown paper.

3. Then Jill came in, and she did grin
   To see Jack's paper plaster;
   Dame Dob, vexed, did whip her next
   For causing Jack's disaster.

# Programming Ideas

**Themes:** siblings; wishes and wishing wells

## Setting the Scene

Ask the students how many of them have brothers and sisters. Name some famous literary characters and ask if they have brothers and sisters. (*example:* Hansel, Cinderella, Little Red Riding Hood, Little Boy Blue, Flopsy, Jill, Paul Bunyan)

## Song ♫ *Jack and Jill*

Tell the students you will be clapping the words to a song. Ask them to guess what the song is. Give hints if necessary. (*example:* This is a famous song about a brother and sister.) Once the children have guessed the song, sing the first verse once, then ask them to try it. Can they sing and clap the words at the same time?

## Story 📖 *Wait and See*

After reading *Wait and See* you might discuss some of the ideas in the story. Ask: "What would you wish for if you had a magic wish? What was Olivia's final wish? Would anyone else wish for a brother or sister? Why would you want a brother or sister? Why not?" Do an informal graph of the number of students who have: brothers, sisters, both, none.

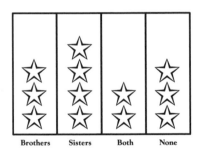

| Brothers | Sisters | Both | None |

## Activities ✏️

### Bulletin Board

Enlarge the wishing well on page 61 for your bulletin board. Read "The Wishing Well" story in *Mouse Tales.* The children can write and post their wishes on the bulletin board.

## *Creative Writing*

Read *Wishing at Dawn in Summer.* As a class or individually, write a "dawning song," (a poem celebrating the beginning of a new day).

## *Craft*

Read *Nobiah's Well.* Make or buy miniature clay pots and paint them with acrylic paints.

## *Movement*

After singing the song, practice "tumbling after." Ask the P.E. teacher to help the children do somersaults either in the classroom or during P.E.

## Books

Carlstrom, Nancy White. *Wishing at Dawn in Summer.* Diane Worfolk Allison, illustrator. Little, Brown, 1992. A brother and sister wish for different things when they go fishing.

Choi, Yangsook. *The Sun Girl and the Moon Boy, a Korean Folktale.* Alfred A. Knopf, 1997. A tiger tries to trick a little boy and girl.

Guthrie, Donna W. *Nobiah's Well, a Modern African Folktale.* Robert Roth, illustrator. Ideals Children's Books, 1993. A young boy shows kindness and is unexpectedly rewarded.

Hill, Eric. *Spot's Baby Sister.* Putnam, 1989. Spot the dog becomes a big brother.

Lobel, Arnold. *Mouse Tales.* Harper & Row, 1972. Seven short stories featuring mice.

Mosel, Arlene. *Tikki Tikki Tembo.* Blair Lent, illustrator. Scholastic, 1968. A little boy almost comes to harm because of his long name.

Munsch, Robert. *Wait and See.* Michael Martchenko, illustrator. Annick Press, 1993. A little girl has her wishes come true with unexpected results.

Standiford, Natalie. *The Best Little Monkeys in the World.* Hilary Knight, illustrator. Random House, 1987. When the parents of two little monkeys go to a party, the youngsters make mischief.

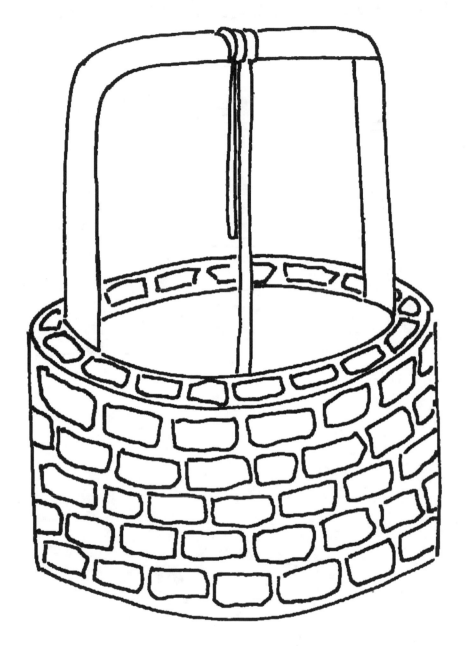

Create a wishing well bulletin board and invite children to add their wishes to the well. Full activity is described on page 60.

# 19
# Little Jack Horner

Lit - tle Jack Hor - ner Sat in a cor - ner,

Eat - ing his Christ - mas pie._____ He stuck in his thumb And

pulled out a plum, And said, "What a good boy am I."_____

# Programming Ideas

**Theme:** pies

## Setting the Scene

Write the word "Dessert" on the board. Ask the children to name some of their favorite desserts and list these on the board. Take a vote to find out the group favorite.

## Song ♫ *Little Jack Horner*

Write the rhyme on the board. Read the verse and ask the children to suggest movements. Write or draw them next to the verse. Try the movements as you slowly say the words. Once the children know them, sing or play the song.

## Story 📖 *Sweet Dream Pie*

After reading this story about a very special pie recipe, ask the children to write their own pie recipes. Make a display so that the children can look at each other's recipe cards. Younger children can draw the ingredients. (*example:* one pie crust, two chocolate bars, three gummy bears.)

## Activities ✏

### *Cooking*

Make pies! Get tart tins, whipped topping, gummy bears, sprinkles, and tiny plastic spoons and let the children assemble their own no-bake pies. *Or* bring in different kinds of fruit and ask the children to identify them. Cut them into small pieces and let the children sample them. Read *We Love Fruit.*

### *Writing*

Enlarge and reproduce the thumb with the plum on page 64. Have each child write an answer to the prompt "I am a good boy/girl because…"

### *Reading/Public Speaking*

Find other Mother Goose rhymes that have to do with pies or make up your own rhymes about pies. Give extra credit or a prize to anyone who memorizes one and recites it for the class.

## *Dramatics*

Make simple costumes to match the book *Pie Rats Ahoy!* You'll need three pirate eye patches (or equivalent props), a poster-size sailing boat (p. 64), a pie tin or picture of a pie (p. 64), a captain's hat, and a crocodile hat (p. 12). Read the book and ask for volunteers to act out the story as you read it again.

## Books

Darling, Benjamin. *Valerie and the Silver Pear.* Dan Lane, illustrator. Four Winds, 1992. A girl and her grandfather make pies and search for a silver pear.

Jackson, Alison. *I Know an Old Lady Who Swallowed a Pie.* Judith Byron Schachner, illustrator. Dutton Children's Books, 1997. A new version of the traditional rhyme featuring an old lady who comes for Thanksgiving dinner.

McCunn, Ruthann Lum. *Pie-Biter.* You-shan Tang, illustrator. Shen's Books, 1983. A young Chinese man works on the railroads and develops a fondness for pies.

Murphy, Stuart J. *A Fair Bear Share.* John Spiers, illustrator. HarperCollins, 1998. Bear cubs collect pie ingredients so they'll get their fair share of a homemade blueberry pie.

Robinson, Fay. *We Love Fruit!* Children's Press, 1992. Nonfiction book about different kinds of fruit and how they grow. Also comes in a big book edition.

Scarry, Richard. *Richard Scarry's Pie Rats Ahoy!* Random House, 1994. Pie rats board Uncle Willy's boat and take his pie.

Wood, Audrey and Mark Teague. *Sweet Dream Pie.* Blue Sky Press, 1998. Ma Brindle makes a gigantic pie for the whole neighborhood.

# Writing and Drama Activities

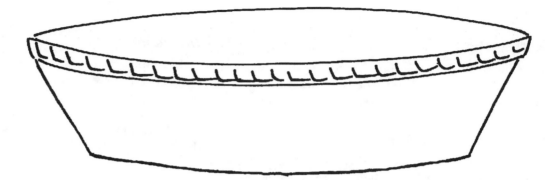

**Pie Tin** Use this illustration with the dramatics activity from page 63.

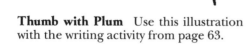

**Thumb with Plum** Use this illustration with the writing activity from page 63.

**Sailing Boat** Use this illustration with the dramatics activity from page 63.

# 20
# Mary, Mary, Quite Contrary

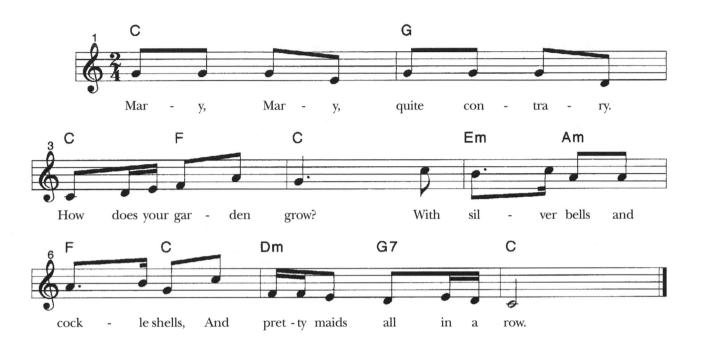

Mar - y, Mar - y, quite con - tra - ry.

How does your gar - den grow? With sil - ver bells and

cock - le shells, And pret - ty maids all in a row.

# Programming Ideas

**Themes:** gardens and gardening

## Setting the Scene

Show pictures of different flowers. Bring in some tools used for gardening: flower seeds, small spade, gloves, watering can. Go through the steps in planting seeds.

## Song ♫ *Mary, Mary, Quite Contrary*

Tell the children that this song is about a little girl who is somewhat stubborn about planting her own garden. After you sing the song a few times, have the children draw and color their own visions of Mary's garden.

## Story 📖 *Wanda's Roses*

Bring in a rosebush or other flowering plant. After reading *Wanda's Roses*, find an area on the school or library grounds to beautify.

## Activities ✏️

### Science/Ecology

Plant a garden either outside or in containers on your windowsill. Read *Compost! Growing Gardens from Your Garbage*. Discuss where you might be able to put a compost bin or pile, and the things the children would be able to put in it. If possible, carry out the plans.

### Craft

Read *Pookins Gets Her Way* and make the children into flowers with Flower Hats (p. 67). *Or* make a flower bed of tissue flowers.

### Art

List the names of flowers that the children know and use the library to find the names a some flowers that are not familiar. Ask each child to select a flower to draw as it really is or an imaginary one that illustrates its name (*example:* snapdragon). Make sure children write the names of the flowers on the back of their drawings. As a class or in pairs go through the cards and guess the flowers. Put the cards where children can look at them more closely or use them as an after-work activity.

### Creative Writing

Read *Thumbelina*. Ask the children to write or draw a new adventure for Thumbelina or one for themselves as a tiny main character.

## Books

Andersen, Hans Christian. *Thumbelina*. A tiny girl has many adventures before finding her tiny prince.

Bjork, Christina. *Linnea's Windowsill Garden*. Joan Sandin, translator. Lena Anderson, illustrator. Farrar, 1988. Linnea tours her indoor garden.

Brisson, Pat. *Wanda's Roses*. Maryann Cocca-Leffler, illustrator. Boyds Mills, 1994. With Wanda's faith and hard work, and some help from her neighbors, she turns an empty lot into a beautiful rose garden.

Cibula, Matt S. *The Contrary Kid*. Brian Strassbug, illustrator. Zino, 1995. Rhymes and cartoons about a kid who enjoys being different.

Coplans, Peta. *Dottie*. Houghton, 1994. A puppy insists on growing a garden.

Cushman, Doug. *Mouse and Mole and the Year-Round Garden*. W.H. Freeman, 1994. A mouse and mole tend their garden.

Glaser, Linda. *Compost! Growing Gardens from Your Garbage*. Anca Hariton, illustrator. Millbrook Press, 1996. A little girl explains how to create a compost that produces rich soil for a garden.

Jeram, Anita. *Contrary Mary*. Candlewick, 1995. Mary, the mouse, wakes up one morning feeling very contrary.

Lester, Helen. *Pookins Gets Her Way*. Lynn Munsinger, illustrator. Houghton Mifflin, 1987. Pookins is used to getting her own way until she meets a magical gnome.

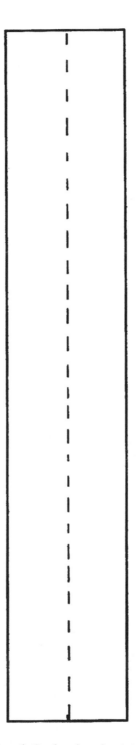

## Flower Hat Instructions

Make the flower hats as part of the craft activity from page 66.

*Materials:* construction paper, scissors, glue, and tape.

*Directions*

1. Cut a 2"-wide band long enough to go around a child's face with a 1½" overlap. Fold in half length-wise.

2. Cut enough petals to cover the length of the band and glue them in place.

3. Fold the other half of the band over and glue it down. Fold petals forward.

4. Wrap around head and tape or staple together.

**petals** Cut enough petals to cover the length of the band.

**band** Cut band so that it is long enough to go around a child's head and have a 1½" overlap.

# 21
# The Muffin Man

1. O do you know the muf - fin man, the
muf - fin man, the muf - fin man? O do you know the
muf - fin man, that lives in Dru - ry Lane?

2. O yes I know the muffin man, etc.

3. O have you seen the muffin man, etc.

4. Where did you see the muffin man, etc.

# Programming Ideas

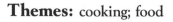

**Themes:** cooking; food

## Setting the Scene

Dip a shoe in flour and leave some footprints around the room. Make a "Wanted" poster like the one below.

WANTED
THE MUFFIN MAN
(aka Mr. Muffy)

Description: Brown Hair,
White puffy hat and apron.
Last seen on Drury Lane.

## Song 🎵 *The Muffin Man*

Walk around carrying the poster. Sing the first verse two or three times and mime asking the children if they know the muffin man. Explain that there are more verses, but it ends in a mystery. Write the first lines of verses two through four on the board. Come up with an ending and then sing the whole song. (*extension:* Write a story based on the song).

## Story 📖 *If You Give a Moose a Muffin*

Book: *If You Give a Moose a Muffin.* After reading the story, make sock puppets using the instructions and pattern on page 70.

## Activities ✏️

### Cooking

Bake a batch of muffins and designate a "muffin man" to deliver them.

### Math

Read *A Dozen Dozens.* Review the concept of dozen and half dozen. Name a dozen friends, a half dozen types of bugs and so on. Could you eat a dozen cookies? How about a half dozen muffins?

### Map Skills

Make up new lyrics based on the streets in your town or near your school. The focus of the song can be a person or a place. (*example:* Oh, do you know the elementary school … that is on Main Street). *Or* read *Roxaboxen* and draw a map to an imaginary town.

### Craft

Make a flipbook for the classroom. Have each child color a self-portrait based on one of the figures on page 70. Collect all the pictures and bind. Cut along the dotted lines so that each third of the page can be turned independently of the rest. Have the children try to identify each other.

## Books

Forest, Heather. *The Baker's Dozen: A Colonial American Tale.* Susan Gaber, illustrator. Harcourt, 1993. A baker learns a lesson after short changing a customer.

Hooper, Meredith. *A Cow, a Bee, a Cookie, and Me.* Alison Bartlett, illustrator. Kingfisher, 1997. A grandmother and her grandson learn all about the making of cookies.

Katzen, Mollie, and Ann Henderson. *Pretend Soup and Other Real Recipes.* Mollie Katzen, illustrator. Tricycle Press, 1994. A children's cookbook with yummy recipes including Hide and Seek Muffins.

McLerran, Alice. *Roxaboxen.* Barbara Cooney, illustrator. Lothrop, Lee & Shepard, 1991. A group of children create an imaginary town.

Numeroff, Laura Joffe. *If You Give a Moose a Muffin.* Felicia Bond, illustrator. HarperCollins, 1991. A moose creates chaos in a boy's house when lured by a muffin.

Spohn, Kate. *Ruth's Bake Shop.* Orchard, 1990. Ruth the octopus spends the day baking.

Van Leeuwen, Jean. *More Tales of Amanda Pig.* Ann Schweninger, illustrator. Dial Books for Young Readers, 1985. Amanda makes bubble bath messes and muffins for dinner.

Ziefert, Harriet. *A Dozen Dozens.* Chris Demarest, illustrator. Viking, 1998. Rhymes and illustrations teach the concept of a dozen and a half a dozen. Math activities included.

# Moose Puppets / Flipbooks

## Moose Puppet

Puppet from *If You Give a Moose a Muffin* story activity on page 69.

*Materials:* brown or tan socks; brown construction paper; buttons; cold heat glue gun or tacky glue; and black felt.

*Directions*

1. Copy antler pattern for template. Place antlers on fold of construction paper and cut.

2. Glue or sew buttons for eyes.

3. Cut out small black felt ovals for nostrils. Glue.

4. Glue or staple antlers in place.

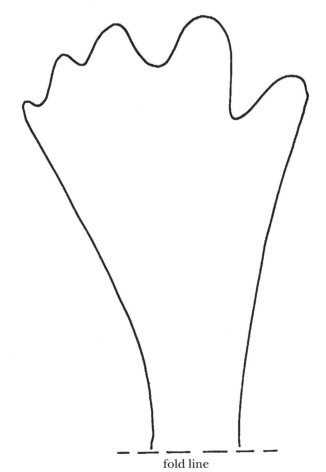

fold line

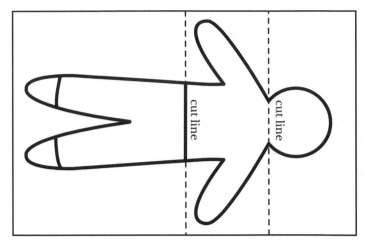

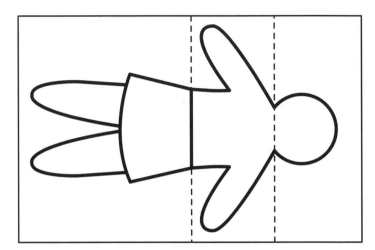

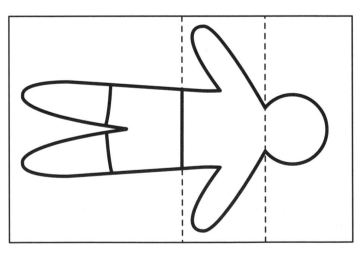

**Flipbook patterns**  Use these figures to make the flipbook from the craft activity on page 69.

# 22
# Oh, Dear, What Can the Matter Be?

# Programming Ideas

**Theme:** circuses; fairs

See Also: *Animal Fair (p. 9)*

## Setting the Scene

Write "fair" and "circus" on the board. (If the children are familiar with school carnivals, write "carnival" on the board, too). Ask: "How many of you have been to a fair? A circus?" Under each word, list some the things the children have seen at each. What is the difference between them? Demonstrate using a dictionary for finding definitions or have older students look up the definitions themselves.

## Song ♫ *Oh, Dear, What Can the Matter Be?*

Start by demonstrating a palms down motion and a palms up motion. When the palms are down, the children are to sit. When the palms are up, the children are to stand. Sing the song line by line. Pause between each line and make the children watch for your hand movements. They should not sit or stand until you have moved your hands. Vary the tempo. End by discussing the song. Ask: "Why was Johnnie so late? Did he bring ribbons? Was she still glad to see him?"

## Story 📖 *Fair!*

After reading the book, ask children to draw a pig, cow, or horse. Have them put their names on the back of the page. Then have an informal county fair and judge the drawings. Award ribbons for each. *Or* read *The Pumpkin Fair*, draw pumpkins, and award ribbons for each.

## Activities ✏️

### Cooking

Hand out popcorn, sit back, and enjoy any of the books listed in the next column. Extension: Decorate small brown bags to make festive containers for the popcorn before distributing it.

### Craft

Read *Circus* by Lois Ehlert and make pinwheels (p. 73).

### Movement

Draw a long line on the ground. Hand a child an umbrella and have them try to walk "the tightrope." Read *Bearymore*.

### Creative Writing

Read *Peter Spier's Circus!* Ask the children to pick one feature of the circus and write a poem or draw a picture. Ask the children to share their work and then read the poetry and look at the pictures in Charles Sullivan's *Circus*. *Or* read *Barnyard Big Top*. As a class or individually, write a letter from Clarence.

## Books

Bunting, Eve. *The Pumpkin Fair*. Eileen Christelow, illustrator. Clarion, 1997. A young girl's little pumpkin earns a ribbon at the pumpkin fair.

Ehlert, Lois. *Circus*. HarperCollins, 1992. Unusual circus members perform for the reader.

Freeman, Don. *Bearymore*. Viking, 1976. A circus bear must come up with a new act.

Kastner, Jill. *Barnyard Big Top*. Simon & Schuster Books for Young Readers, 1997. Uncle Julius sets up a circus in a front yard and acquires an unusual performer.

Lewin, Ted. *Fair!* Lothrop, Lee & Shepard, 1997. Wonderful illustrations and descriptions of a county fair.

Spier, Peter. *Peter Spier's Circus!* Doubleday Books for Young Readers, 1992. Peter Spier's characteristic illustrations bring a circus to life.

Sullivan, Charles, *Circus*. Rizzoli International, 1992. Poems, paintings, and photographs celebrate the circus.

Watson, Clyde. *Applebet: An ABC*. Wendy Watson, illustrator. Farrar, Straus and Giroux, 1982. Follow an apple and a little girl to and from a county fair.

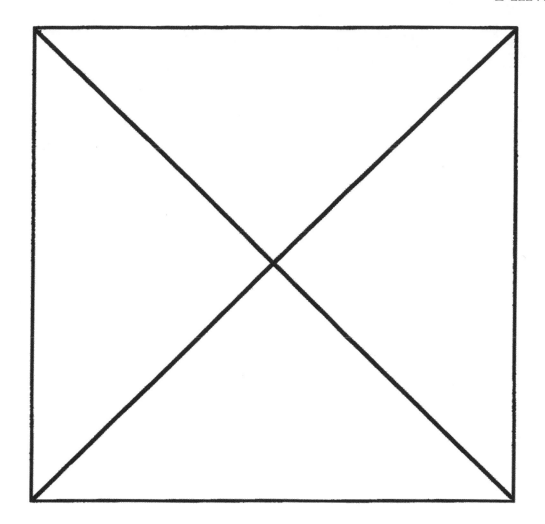

**Pinwheel** (from craft activity on p. 72)

*Materials:* white or colored lightweight paper; scissors; new pencils with erasers; dressmaker's pins; and glue.

*Directions*

1. Enlarge the pattern. Cut the diagonal lines almost to the center.

2. Place a little glue in the center of the pinwheel and pull one corner into the center. Continue to glue the left corner of each triangle on top of the previous one. Dry.

3. Punch a pin in the center of the pinwheel and into the eraser of a pencil. *Blow!*

# 23
# This Old Man

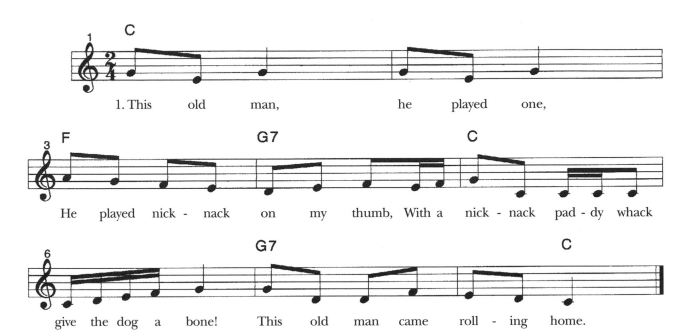

1. This old man, he played one,
He played nick - nack on my thumb, With a nick - nack pad - dy whack give the dog a bone! This old man came roll - ing home.

2. This old man, he played two,
He played nick-nack on my shoe.

3. This old man, he played three,
He played nick-nack on my knee.

4. This old man, he played four,
He played nick-nack on my door.

5. This old man, he played five,
He played nick-nack on my hive.

6. This old man, he played six,
He played nick-nack on my sticks.

7. This old man, he played sev'n,
He played nick-nack till elev'n.

8. This old man, he played eight,
He played nick-nack on my gate.

9. This old man, he played nine,
He played nick-nack on my spine.

10. This old man, he played ten,
He played nick-nack over again.

# Programming Ideas

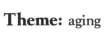

**Theme:** aging

## Setting the Scene

"You can't teach an old dog new tricks." Ask: "What do you think this means? Is it true? Does it apply to people?"

## Song ♫ *This Old Man*

Ask: "Who knows the song? Can anyone demonstrate the movements?" If no one knows any movements, make up something to use on the section, "With a nick nack paddy whack give the dog a bone, This old man came rolling home." Review the verses, and then sing the song together.

## Story 📖 *Amos: The Story of an Old Dog and His Couch*

After reading the story about Amos, give the children a copy of the sofa picture on page 76 so they can draw themselves on it. Have them color and cut out these self portraits. Then using old magazines as a source, have children paste their sofa picture on a photograph of someplace they would like to go.

## Activities ✏️

### Poetry

Read some of the poems from *There Was an Old Man…A Gallery of Nonsense Rhymes*. Each child can illustrate one of the rhymes from the book or write and illustrate one his own. *Or* read *There Was an Old Woman Who Lived in a Glove*. Pick out different items around the classroom and make up your own rhymes. A classroom book can be created from either activity.

### Homework

Ask a grandparent or other adult for an interesting or funny story that happened to them when they were children. Have the children draw or illustrate the story and then give it back to the adult as a gift.

### Writing/Goals

Ask the children to draw a picture of themselves on one side of the page and a picture of their grown-up self on the other. Ask them to write or draw some of the things they want to do or see between now and then.

### Problem-Solving

Read *The Old Woman and Her Pig*. Brainstorm some serious and funny ways of getting the pig over the stile. Award a prize to anyone who makes or draws an invention to solve the problem.

## Books

Ackerman, Karen. *Song and Dance Man*. Stephen Gammell, illustrator. Scholastic, 1988. In this Caldecott winner, Grandpa shares his old vaudeville act.

Lear, Edward. *There Was an Old Man… A Gallery of Nonsense Rhymes*. Michele Lemieux, illustrator. Morrow Junior Books, 1994. A collection of humorous poetry.

Litzinger, Rosanne. *The Old Woman and Her Pig: An Old English Tale*. Harcourt Brace Jovanovich, 1993. An old lady tries to get help in getting her pig over the stile.

Lodge, Bernard. *There Was an Old Woman Who Lived in a Glove*. Whispering Coyote Press, 1992. The old woman who lived in a glove goes exploring.

Seligson, Susan, and Howie Schneider. *Amos: The Story of an Old Dog and His Couch*. Little, Brown, 1987. An old dog discovers a new way to travel.

Winch, John. *The Old Man Who Loved to Sing*. Scholastic, Inc., 1993. An old man moves to the country so he can hear his music.

Winch, John. *The Old Woman Who Loved to Read*. Holiday House, 1996. An old woman moved to the country believing she would have a lot of time to read.

Wright, Jill. *The Old Woman and the Willy Nilly Man*. Glen Rounds, illustrator. G.P. Putnam, 1987. The Willy Nilly Man plays a trick on an old woman, but she gets even.

# Couch

After reading *Amos: The Story of an Old Dog and His Couch* (p.75) have children create their own travelling couch using the pattern here.

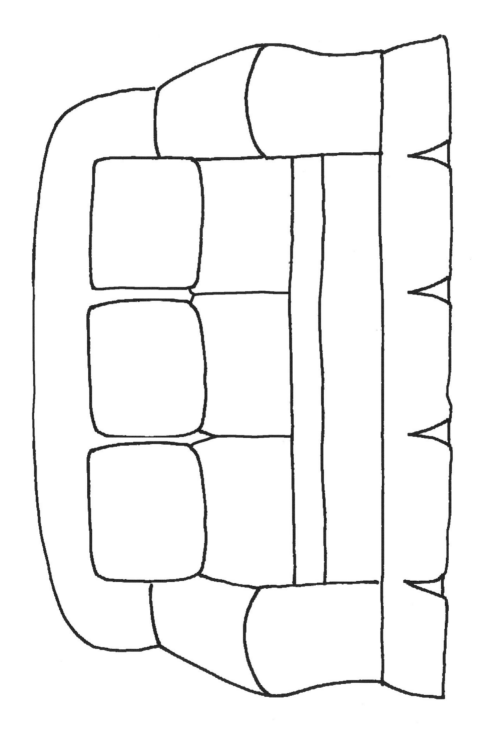

# 24
# To Market, To Market

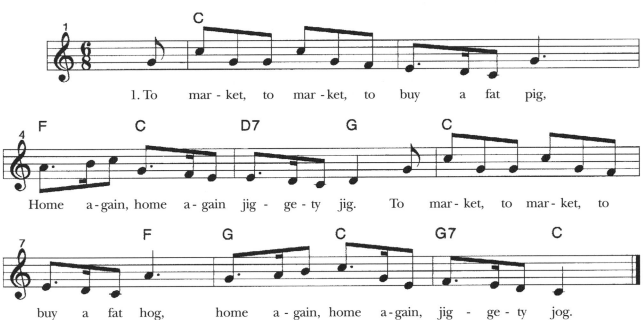

1. To mar - ket, to mar - ket, to buy a fat pig,
Home a - gain, home a - gain jig - ge - ty jig. To mar - ket, to mar - ket, to
buy a fat hog, home a - gain, home a - gain, jig - ge - ty jog.

2. To market, to market, to buy a plum bun,
   Home again, home again, market is done.

# Programming Ideas

**Themes:** cooking; food

## Setting the Scene

Set up a corner of the room as a market. Bring in fruit and vegetables (real or fake), or paste pictures of food on large index cards. Ask your students if they have ever gone to the grocery store. Have them describe the store and their experience. Then explain what a market is, listing the differences between a market and a grocery store. (*examples:* markets are usually open air, they have individual sellers, and produce is usually not packaged)

## Song ♫ *To Market, To Market*

Play a modified version of Musical Chairs. Arrange chairs in a circle. There should be enough chairs for every child except two. Ask for one student to come up with you to help you sing and to act as judge. Sing the song once while the other students walk or skip around the room. On the word "jog" everyone needs to find a seat. The person left standing becomes the new judge. (Note: If there is an argument over who reached a chair first, the judge picks a number between 1 and 10 and the one closest to the judge's number becomes the new judge).

## Story 📖 *Marti & the Mango*

Write the following note on a large piece of paper and read it to the class: "Dinner Tonight at My House. Bring a mango. Gomez."

Ask: "Does anyone know what a mango is? Can you describe it? What does it taste like?" This is a story about a mouse who discovers just that. With small note pads or paper, have the children write down information about a mango as it is revealed in the story. Or on completion of the story, go over the information as a group.

## Activities ✏️

### Math

Read The Shopping Basket. Ask: "How many eggs were left when Steven got home? Bananas? Apples? Oranges? Doughnuts? Chips?" Or bring in a basket with fruit or other items to count, add and subtract.

### Craft

Read *Grandma Went to Market.* Make the masks on page 79 or the lanterns on page 80.

### Cooking

Read *Market Day* or *Market*. Bring in some fruits and vegetables, including exotic ones, for the children to see and taste. Look at the glossary in *Marti and the Mango*. Make comparisons between the exotic foods and the more familiar ones.

## Books

Blackstone, Stella. *Grandma Went to the Market: A Round-the-World Counting Rhyme.* Bernard Lodge, illustrator. Houghton Mifflin, 1996. Follow the international shopping adventures of grandma.

Bunting, Eve. *Market Day.* Holly Berry, illustrator. HarperCollins, 1996. A young girl is given a penny to spend at the market in an Irish town.

Burningham, John. *The Shopping Basket.* Candlewick, 1980. On the way home from the market, a boy uses his wiles to outsmart some threatening animals.

Lewin, Ted. *Market!* Lothrop, 1996. Shares, in bright colors, some of the excitement in markets from around the world.

Medearis, Angela Shelf. *Rum-a-Tum-Tum.* James E. Ransome, illustrator. Holiday, 1997. The markets in the French Quarter of New Orleans.

Miranda, Anne. *To Market, To Market.* Janet Stevens, illustrator. Harcourt, 1997. A revised version of the rhyme where the shopper gets more than she bargained for.

Moreton, Daniel. *Marti & the Mango.* Stewart, Tabori, & Chang, 1993. Marti, the mouse, with the help of his friends learns what a mango is.

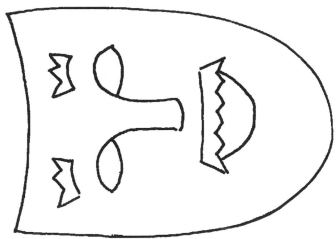

## Mask Instructions

The mask patterns at left are part of the craft activity from page 78.

*Materials:* colored construction paper; crayons or markers; elastic; and reinforcing paper rings.

*Directions*

1. Enlarge patterns to create templates.

2. Color and decorate masks with crayons or markers.

3. Cut out eyes and mouths.

4. Punch two holes on the side and reinforce with stickers (or clear wrapping tape) on both sides. Better yet, laminate!

5. Measure elastic, run through holes and tie.

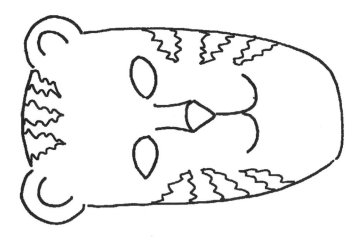

# Lanterns

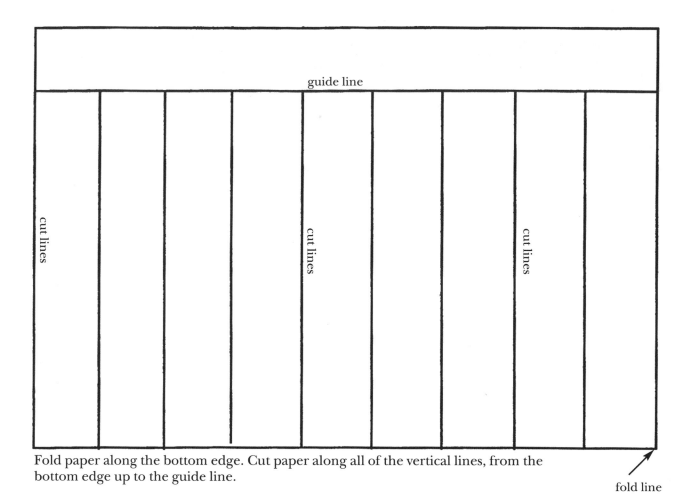

guide line

cut lines

cut lines

cut lines

Fold paper along the bottom edge. Cut paper along all of the vertical lines, from the bottom edge up to the guide line.

fold line

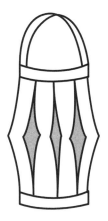

## Lantern Instructions

The lantern is part of the craft activity from page 78.

*Materials:* construction paper; scissors; glue or stapler.

*Directions*

1. Using pattern as a guide, fold construction paper in half. Mark lines from folded edge, leaving a ½" border from the other edge and draw a guide line.

2. Cut up to the guide line in even widths. Open.

3. Turning the lantern lengthwise, overlap just the edges and glue or staple together.

4. Cut a handle and attach.

**handle**

# 25
# Did You Ever See a Lassie?

Did you ev - er see a lass - ie, a lass - ie, a

lass - ie? Did you ev - er see a lass - ie go

this way and that? Go this way and that way, and

this way and that way? Did you ev - er see a

lass - ie go this way and that?

# Programming Ideas

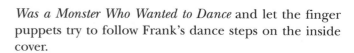

**Theme:** dances and dancing

## Setting the Scene

Ask: "What would you do if you couldn't watch TV?" List the answers. "Would any of you dance? Why or why not? What kind of dancing would you do?"

## Song 🎵 *Did You Ever See a Lassie?*

Sing or play the song as the children play a variation of the game Duck Duck Goose.

To Play the Game: Have children sit in a circle or any formation. Choose a child to be "it." The child who is "it" dances in and out among the children in any direction or pattern and taps them on the head. Whoever is tapped on the last word, ("that") is the next "it." (Note: If a boy is "it," change the words of the song to "Did You Ever See a Laddie?").

## Story 📖 *Twist with a Burger, Jitter with a Bug* or *Can You Dance, Dalila?*

Write the word "Dance" on the board. Brainstorm a list of words that have to do with dance (*examples:* ballet, boogie, jazz, gymnastics, toes). Read one of the books above, then ask the children if they can add any other words to the list of dances. Bring in recordings of different styles of music and let the children move to the music.

## Activities ✏️

### Movement

Ask the P.E. or music teacher if they teach any dances. If so, could they show one to your class this week? *Or* bring in some filmy fabrics and streamers for the children to dance with. *Or* hold a dance contest.

### Craft

Make finger puppets (p. 83) and then let the children make their puppets dance along to music. Read *Frank Was a Monster Who Wanted to Dance* and let the finger puppets try to follow Frank's dance steps on the inside cover.

### Science/Birds

Discuss birds and how they move. Watch a video of birds or go outside and observe. Try to mimic their movements, then read *Silent Lotus.*

### Art

Read *Color Dance.* Discuss color mixing and experiment with water colors. Extension: Discuss colors and emotions.

## Books

de Paola, Tomie. *Oliver Button Is a Sissy.* Harcourt Brace Jovanovich, 1979. Oliver persists in dancing despite teasing.

Graves, Keith. *Frank Was a Monster Who Wanted to Dance.* Chronicle Books, 1999. A monster dances on stage.

Jonas, Ann. *Color Dance.* Greenwillow Books, 1989. Dancers show color combinations.

Kroll, Virginia. *Can You Dance, Dalila?* Nancy Carpenter, illustrator. Simon & Schuster Books for Young Readers, 1996. Dalila tries many kinds of dances before she finds the one for her.

Lee, Jeanne M. *Silent Lotus.* Farrar, Straus & Giroux, 1991. Lotus becomes a famous dancer even though she cannot hear or speak.

Lowery, Linda. *Twist with a Burger, Jitter with a Bug.* Pat Dypold, illustrator. Houghton Mifflin, 1995. Rhythmic rhymes full of dance words.

Martin, Bill Jr., and John Archambault. *Barn Dance!* Ted Rand, illustrator. Henry Holt, 1986. A boy attends an unusual barn dance.

Mathers, Petra. *Sophie and Lou.* HarperCollins, 1991. A shy mouse teaches herself how to dance.

# Finger Puppets

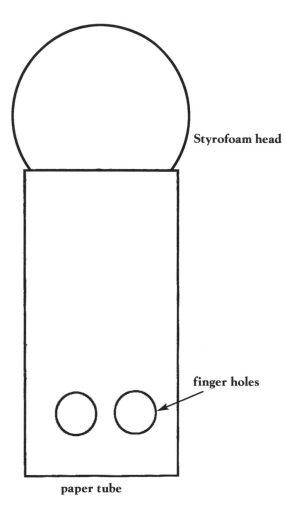

**Styrofoam head**

**finger holes**

**paper tube**

## Finger Puppet Instructions

*Materials:* paper tubes, Styrofoam balls, construction paper, yarn, glue, and markers.

*Directions*

1. Cut tubes to be approximately 4" high. Wrap with construction paper.

2. Punch out two holes for fingers.

3. Glue head in place. Cut out arms and glue them in place.

4. Add facial features with markers and glue on hair to complete puppet.

**arm (cut 2)**

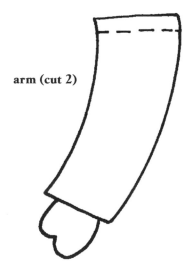

# 26
# Lightly Row

1.Light - ly row, light - ly row,

o'er the shin - ing waves we go; Smooth - ly glide,

smooth - ly glide, on the si - lent tide.

Let the winds and wa - ters be min - gled with our

mel - o - dy, Sing and float, sing and float,

in our lit - tle boat.

2. Far away, far away, echo in the rocks at play,
Calling not, calling not, to this lonely spot.
Only with the sea bird's note shall our dying music float,
Lightly row, lightly row, echo's voice is low.

3. Happy we, full of glee, sailing o'er the wavy sea,
Happy we, full of glee, sailing o'er the sea,
Luna sheds her clearest light, stars are sparkling, twinkling bright,
Happy we, full of glee, sailing o'er the sea.

# Programming Ideas

**Themes:** boats; water

## Setting the Scene

Cut out different types of boats from magazines or reproduce boat pictures on page 86. Talk with the children about the different kinds of boats and their uses. Classify them into boats that have motors and boats that don't: tugboats, ferries, fishing boats vs. canoes, kayaks, rowboats.

## Song ♫ *Lightly Row*

Have the children sit in pairs (one behind the other) and pretend they are in a boat rowing as they sing the song.

## Story 📖 *Jiro's Pearl*

Make a good luck goldfish using the pattern on page 87. Discuss the concept of symbols and symbolism. Name some animals and what they symbolize (*examples:* goldfish—good fortune; lion—strength; lamb—gentleness).

### Good Luck Goldfish Instructions

*Materials:* orange, yellow, blue and green construction paper; glue; scissors; fishing line; and a tapestry needle.

*Directions*

1. Enlarge the pattern for a template.
2. Cut out the parts.
3. Glue fins to fish body on dotted line. Glue along the outer edge and place on fish body.
4. Starting at the tail, glue a row of scales (glue just the top of scale). Repeat to just above the fins.
5. Glue on the eyes.
6. Using fishing line and a needle, pierce fish mouth and tie a knot.
7. Pierce a pearl and slide it on the line, down to the mouth of the fish. (optional)

## Activities ✏️

### Music/Dramatics

Read *Row, Row, Row Your Boat* by Pippi Goodhart. Sing and act out the wonderful new rhymes to this classic song.

### Art

Read *Boat Ride with Lillian Two Blossom.* Talk about Native American beliefs and folklore: nature and animal spirits. Let the children draw and color great spirit fish for the room.

### Creative Writing

Have the children draw a picture or write a story about a boat ride. Add a prompt if necessary using superlatives like fastest, slowest, smallest, or largest (*example:* If I had the fastest boat in the world, I would…).

### Graphing

Read *Row, Row, Row Your Boat* by Joanne Oppenheim. List the boats the children would most like to be on and make an informal graph by listing the children's names under the boats they prefer.

## Books

Allen, Pamela. *Who Sank the Boat?* Putnam, 1996. Someone among five animals is guilty of sinking the boat.

Barton, Bryon. *Boats.* HarperCollins, 1986. Boldly illustrated board book about different types of boats and the work they do.

Challoner, Jack. *Floating and Sinking.* Raintree, 1996. Simple illustrations and hands-on activities are provided to explain the qualities of things that float and those that don't.

Goodhart, Pippa. *Row, Row, Row Your Boat.* Stephen Lambert, illustrator. Crown, 1997. Two children and a stuffed rabbit have a lively adventure in their rowboat. Song included.

Oppenheim, Joanne. *Row, Row, Row Your Boat.* Kevin O'Malley, illustrator. Bantam, 1993. Starting off in the tub, a boy navigates through varied waters and ships.

Polacco, Patricia. *Boat Ride with Lillian Two Blossom.* Philomel, 1988. An Indian woman takes two children on a strange and wonderful boat ride.

Powers, Daniel. *Jiro's Pearl.* Candlewick Press, 1997. A young Japanese boy experiences an unusual adventure when he sets off in a boat to get his grandmother's medicine.

# Boats

Enlarge and cut out the different kinds of boats here to set the scene for "Lightly Row" on page 85.

# Good Luck Goldfish

Directions for making the Good Luck Goldfish are on p.85 in the story activity.

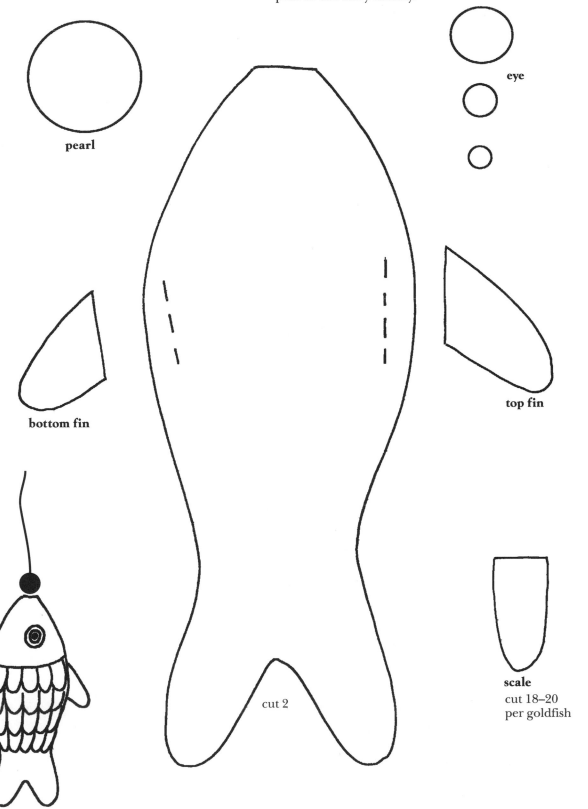

pearl

eye

bottom fin

top fin

scale

cut 18–20
per goldfish

cut 2

# 27
# London Bridge

1. Lon - don Bridge is fall - ing down, fall - ing down, fall - ing down.

Lon - don Bridge is fall - ing down, My fair la - dy.

2. Build it up with iron bars, iron bars, iron bars,
   Build it up with iron bars, My fair lady.

3. Iron bars will bend and break, bend and break, bend and break,
   Iron bars will bend and break, My fair lady.

4. Build it up with silver and gold, silver and gold, silver and gold,
   Build it up with silver and gold, My fair lady.

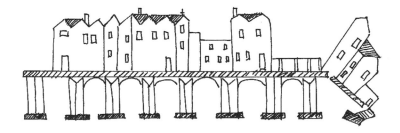

*London Bridge was built in 1209 and crossed the Thames River. It was built out of brick and wood and had houses, inns and shops on it. It was destroyed by fire and replaced in 1831.*

# Programming Ideas

**Themes:** bridges; London

## Setting the Scene

Bring in pictures of London (a travel agent will have brochures) and make a bulletin board. Make sure you include a map with "London" marked in big letters and a flag. Include some of the well-known sights: Big Ben, Tower of London, and London Bridge.

## Song ♫ *London Bridge*

Form a bridge by having the children face each other in two rows, holding hands up in the air. As you sing the song, the first two children in the lines drop their hands and walk through the bridge. When they are through, they stay at the end and raise their hands again to form the bridge. Then the next two children follow and so on until everyone in the line has gone through the bridge.

## Story 📖 *London Bridge Is Falling Down*

Talk about the history of London Bridge and distribute pictures (p. 90) for children to color.

## Activities ✏️

### Science

Build bridges using blocks or Legos and read *Bridges Are to Cross.* Build new bridges.

### Craft

Read *The Bells of London.* Make bells out of cans (using different-sized cans and wooden beads) to ring to the rhymes.

#### Bell Directions

*Materials:* soup cans, twine or cord, wooden beads

1. Collect soup cans (cleaned and covers removed).
2. Using a hammer and large nail, punch a hole in the bottom of the can.
3. Cut twine or cord approximately 8" long. String the cord through the bead and tie to secure.
4. Pull the other end of the cord through the hole in the can and knot it so that bead will strike the side of the can. Cut off excess.

### Movement

Play London Bridge Limbo. Two children hold hands in the air to form a bridge. The rest of the children, one at a time, go under the bridge in limbo style singing. The bridge is lowered after all the children have gone through and it repeats until only one child is left. That child then chooses a partner to help form the bridge and the game starts over.

### Cooking

Makes scones and have a tea party.

#### English Scones

- 2 c. self-rising flour
- 1 tsp. salt
- 9 Tbs. margarine or butter
- ¼ c. brown sugar
- raisins
- milk, approx. 8 ozs.

Mix flour and salt in bowl. Mix in butter with hands until fine crumbs form. Mix in sugar and raisins. Add milk, a little at a time, to make a soft dough. Knead on a lightly floured surface. Roll ¾" thick and stamp out rounds with a small biscuit cutter or glass. Bake at 425 degrees on lightly greased pan for 10 to 15 minutes. Makes 20 regular-sized scones.

## Books

Bemelmans, Ludwig. *Madeline in London.* Viking, 1961. Madeline's adventure in London and the rescue of a horse.

Carter, Polly. *The Bridge Book.* Roy Doty, illustrator. Simon & Schuster, 1992. The evolution and construction of bridges.

Rogers, Paul. *From Me to You.* Jane Johnson, illustrator. Orchard, 1988. A grandmother tells her granddaughter of her life in an English family.

Spier, Peter (illustrator). *London Bridge Is Falling Down.* Doubleday, 1985. Rhyme and song which includes historical information.

Sturges, Philemon. *Bridges Are to Cross.* Giles Laroche, illustrator. Putnam, 1998. Different types of bridges and their uses are explained.

Wolff, Ashley. *The Bells of London.* Dodd, Mead, 1985. The activities of London in the 1800s accompany the traditional rhymes of church bells.

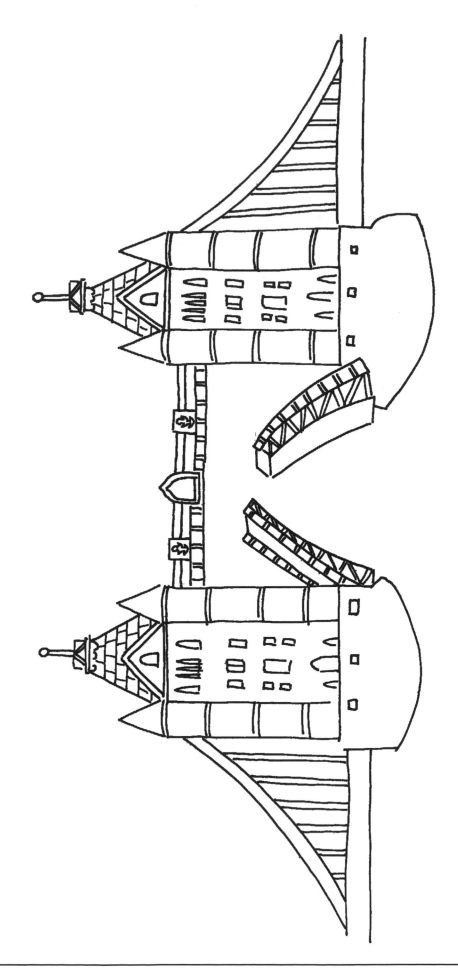

**London Bridge**

# 28
# Looby Loo

Here we go loo - by loo, Here we go loo - by light,

Here we go loo - by loo, All on a Sat - ur - day night. _____ (1.) I

put my right hand in, _____ I put my right hand

out, _____ I give my right hand a shake, shake, shake, and

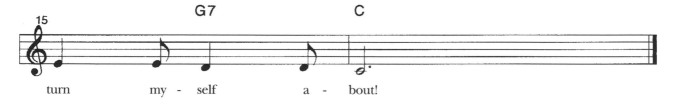

turn my - self a - bout!

2. I put my left hand in, etc.

3. I put my right foot in, etc.

4. I put my left foot in, etc.

5. I put my head right in, etc.

6. I put my whole self in, etc.

# Programming Ideas

**Themes:** bathtime; body

See Also: *Rub-a-Dub-Dub (p. 101)*

## Setting the Scene

Discuss the days of the week, asking children if their families have any activities reserved for a particular day? Answers might include church on Sundays, dance class on Wednesdays, and pizza for supper on Fridays. Tell children that a long time ago, many people would take their baths on Saturday nights (*They only took baths once a week!*) and children would sing "Looby Loo" as they washed up.

## Song ♫ *Looby Loo*

Make up movements to the chorus or use the movements below. Sing and move to the song.

> **Movements for "Looby Loo"**
>
> *Stand in a circle.*
>
> Here we go looby loo
> (*turn to the right and clap*)
>
> Here we go looby light
> (*turn to the left and clap*)
>
> Here we go looby loo
> (*turn to the right and clap*)
>
> All on a Saturday night.
> (*turn to the left and clap*)

## Story 📖 *King Bidgood's in the Bathtub* and *Andrew's Bath*

Ask: "How many of you like to take baths? How many don't?" The first story is about someone who likes to take baths and the second story is about someone who didn't. After reading both stories, have the children brainstorm ways to get King Bidgood out of the tub and Andrew into the tub. Hand out copies of the bathtub on page 93 and ask the children to illustrate their favorite idea. (Note: A longer but classic story about a girl who didn't like to take baths is "The Radish Cure" in *Mrs. Piggle Wiggle.*)

## Activities ✏️

### Science/Music

Add verses to practice using vocabulary for parts of the body (*examples:* "Put your cranium in …") and perform them.

### Creative Writing

Reinforce days of the week by reading *Dinosaur Days* and writing stories beginning with the prompt, "What if on Monday …." *Or* for fun, read *Heckedy Peg* and retell the story by changing the wishes of the children and the food they become (*example:* Monday could want jelly and she turns into a peanut butter sandwich).

### Game

Read *Seven Blind Mice.* Blindfold seven children and let them touch an object and guess what it is.

### Art/Movement

Reinforce parts of the body by reading and doing the movements to *The Little Old Lady Who Was Not Afraid of Anything.* Extension: The scary figure in the book turns out to be a scarecrow. What if it was a monster? Ask the children to draw two shoes, a pair of pants, a shirt, two gloves, a hat, and a head to go with a monster or animal of their choice. Share the pictures and retell the first story or read *Frank Was a Monster Who Wanted to Dance.*

## Book

Graves, Keith. *Frank Was a Monster Who Wanted to Dance.* Chronicle Books, 1999. A monster dances on stage.

Manning, Linda. *Dinosaur Days.* Vlasta Van Kampen, illustrator. BridgeWater Books, 1993. Dinosaurs come into a girl's house each day of the week.

MacDonald, Betty. *Mrs. Piggle Wiggle.* Hilary Knight, illustrator. Harper & Row, 1947. A series of stories featuring a woman who can cure any child's misbehavior.

McPhail, David. *Andrew's Bath.* Little, Brown, 1984. Andrew finally takes a bath "all by himself."

Williams, Linda. *The Little Old Lady Who Was Not Afraid of Anything.* Megan Lloyd, illustrator. Harper & Row, 1986. A little old lady is almost frightened on her walk home.

Wood, Audrey. *Heckedy Peg.* Don Wood, illustrator. Harcourt Brace Jovanovich, 1987. A mother must save her children from a witch.

———. *King Bidgood's in the Bathtub.* Don Wood, illustrator. Harcourt Brace Jovanovich, 1985. A king doesn't want to leave his bath.

Young, Ed. *Seven Blind Mice.* Scholastic, 1992. Seven blind mice meet an elephant.

# Bath Tub

Reproduce the bath tub to use with the story activity from page 92 or the art activity from page 102.

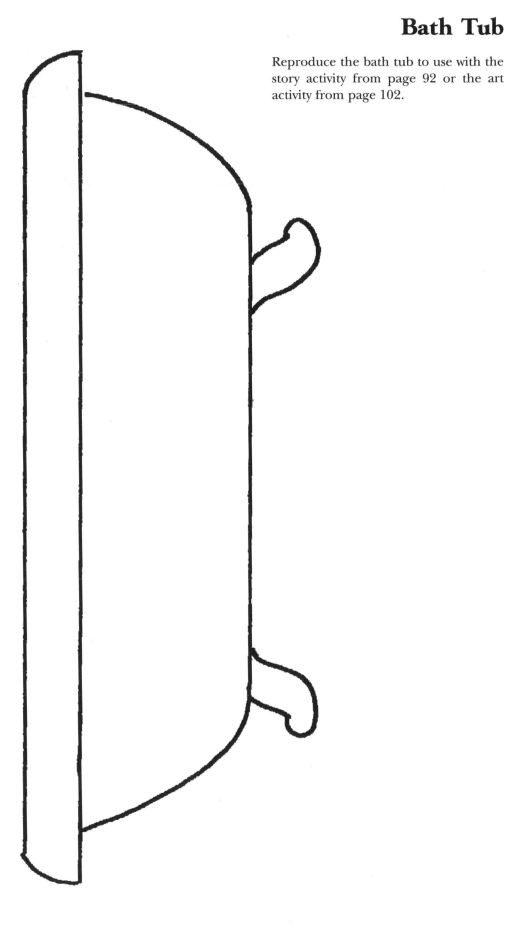

# 29

# New River Train

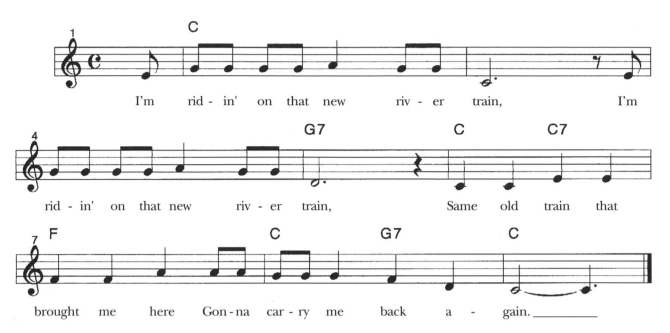

I'm  rid - in'  on  that  new  riv - er  train,  I'm
rid - in'  on  that  new  riv - er  train,  Same  old  train  that
brought  me  here  Gon - na  car - ry  me  back  a - gain._____

# Programming Ideas

**Theme:** trains

## Setting the Scene

Dress up as a conductor or an engineer (with whistle if possible). Meet the children at the door and invite them to "come aboard." Hand each a ticket as they enter the room. (The ticket can be as simple as a slip of blank construction paper). Today the children are passengers on the "New River Train," and they need to keep up with their tickets all day. Punch the tickets after the children are seated and punch them each time the class returns to the room (after lunch for example). Those children who still have their tickets at the end of the day can have an extra "train treat" or prize of some sort.

## Song ♫ *New River Train*

Ask: "What do you think of when I say this: Clickety clack, clickety clack, chugga chugga choo choo." (A train). "Can anyone show us how to move like a train might move?"

Pick a child to be the conductor. As the class sings the song, the conductor moves around the room and taps another child by the end of the song. The new child becomes the conductor.

## Story 📖 *The Train Ride*

Share *The Train Ride* with the class. Then, as a class, in small groups, or individually, write your own train journey stories in the same format as the book or with this simpler prompt: "I'm here on a train ride, what will I see? _____ That's what I see." (Note: Encourage the children to use their imaginations. The train journeys do not need to be limited to the countryside, a country or even a planet. *Or* if you are studying a geographical region, the stories can be limited to a region).

## Activities ✏

### Bulletin Board

Read *Trains* or *The Little Engine that Could*. Copy and enlarge train cars on page 97 so that each is the size of an 8½" x 11" sheet of paper. Put the engine on a bulletin board or high on the wall. Make a copy of the train car for each child. Have the children color their car and draw some sort of cargo. Some children can even design specialty cars, such as rack cars for automobiles. Put the cars up on the wall and place the caboose at the end.

### Craft

Read *The Train* by David McPhail and make engineer caps (pattern and instructions on p. 96). You may want to have volunteers to help children fit and assemble their caps.

### Research

Using a graphic organizer like a web or a diagram, list what the children know about trains. As a class, read *Trains* and add to the list.

### Creative Writing

Reproduce the picture of the engine on page 99. Write "I Think I Can" across the top before copying it for each child. The children can write or draw something they would like to learn how to do. Color.

## Books

Better Homes and Gardens. *Trains and Railroads.* Meredith Corporation, 1991. Art, craft, cooking, science, and nature activities.

Crebbin, June. *The Train Ride.* Stephen Lambert, illustrator. Candlewick Press, 1995. A child enjoys a train ride in rhyme.

Gibbons, Gail. *Trains.* Holiday House, 1987. Present bright, informative drawings of trains.

Hagen, Jeff. *Hiawatha Passing.* Kenneth Shue, illustrator. Henry Holt, 1995. A boy is awakened by a passing train.

London, Jonathan. *The Owl Who Became the Moon.* Ted Rand, illustrator. Dutton Children's Books, 1993. A boy imagines a train ride through the forest at night.

McPhail, David. *The Train.* Little, Brown, 1977. At night, a young boy fixes and then takes a ride on his toy train.

Piper, Watty. *The Little Engine that Could.* George and Doris Hauman, illustrators. Platt & Munk, 1930. A little engine successfully crosses over a mountain to deliver goodies to children.

Temple, Charles. *Train.* Larry Johnson, illustrator. Houghton Mifflin, 1996. A family takes a ride on the C & O Train.

# Engineer Caps

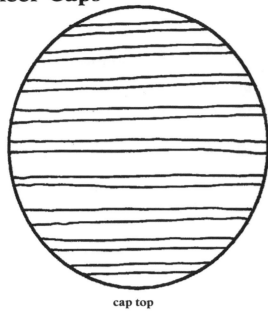

**cap top**

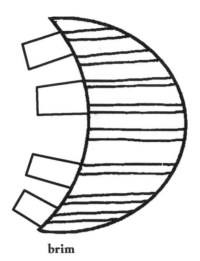

**brim**

**band**

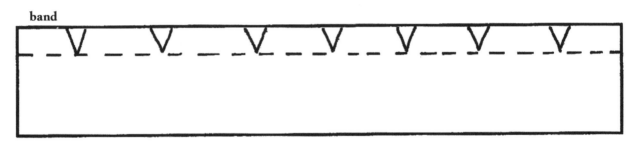

## Engineer Cap Instructions

The engineer cap is from the craft activity for the "New River Train" on page 95.

*Materials:* Blue or gray construction paper; scissors; glue; and a black marker.

*Directions*

1. Enlarge the pattern to create a template. Cut cap top and brim.

2. Cut a band approximately 2" wide. The length will be determined by measuring the circumference of the circle plus ½" for overlap. Draw stripes (optional).

3. Draw a fold line on the band (approx. ½" from the edge). Fold.

4. Cut gussets out of the band (see illustration).

5. On the wrong side of the cap, place glue around the edge. Carefully glue the trimmed and folded edge of the band to the cap top. Fold the tabs up on the brim and glue or tape them to the inside of the brim.

# Train Cars

Enlarge and color the train cars to create the bulletin board for the "New River Train" from page 95.

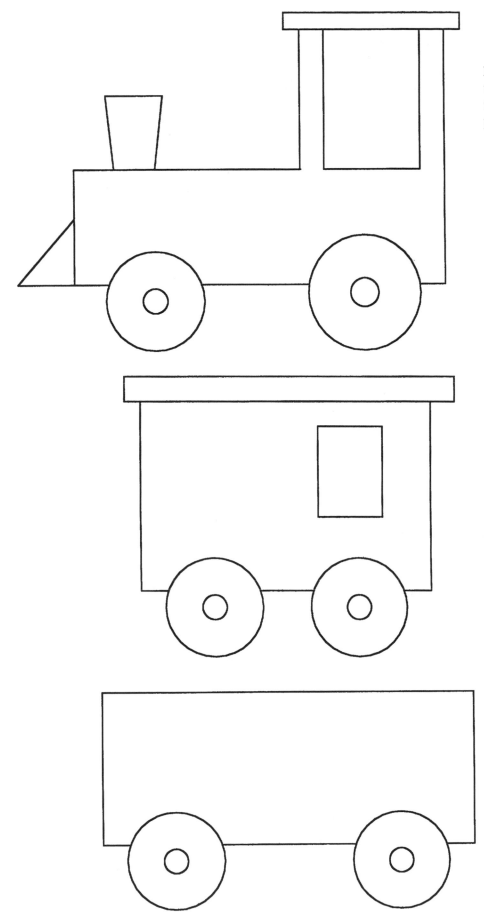

# 30
# Rig a Jig Jig

2. A pretty girl I chanced to meet,
   chanced to meet, chanced to meet,
   A pretty girl I chanced to meet,
   Hi-ho, hi-ho, hi-ho.

# Programming Ideas

**Themes:** community; travel

## Setting the Scene

Ask: "How many of you like to go for walks? Why or why not?" Explain that one reason you like to go for walks is that you never know who you will meet or what you will see. Ask the children what they might see on a walk in the country. What might they see on a walk in the city?

## Song ♫ *Rig a Jig Jig*

Explain that the song is about walking down a street and meeting a pretty girl or a handsome boy. Sing or play the song once, then play the game, changing the words to the song slightly. (Instead of "pretty girl" say something like "charming friend" or "new best friend.")

Game: Sit or stand in a circle. A person walks around the circle until he/she finds someone to "rig a jig jig" with. When the chorus of the song starts, the two grab hands and skip around the circle. When the chorus is over, the original person returns to the circle while the new person walks around during the verse. Variation: Everyone walks around at random. Pause between the verse and the chorus until everyone finds a partner. (The odd person out can "rig a jig jig" with the teacher or form a threesome). The pairs (or threesome) hold hands and skip around during the chorus. At the end of the chorus, they drop hands and move around alone as the verse is repeated.

## Story 📖 *Around Town*

After reading the book, close it deliberately. Challenge the children to name ten or more people or things the mother and daughter saw on the city streets. (If they meet the challenge, perhaps they could be rewarded with extra time on the playground or another privilege).

## Activities ✏️

### Music

Read *Max Found Two Sticks.* Ask the music teacher for drumming activities or accompany a song or recording with pencils on the edge of the desks.

### Poetry

Read *Shrek!* Discuss what he saw on his walk. As a class or individually, write a poem about the walk. Older children might try writing their own versions of the love poetry between Shrek and the princess.

### Game

Discuss exaggerations and rumors. Play the Exaggeration Game which is based on *And to Think I Saw It on Mulberry Street.* Write the phrase "horse and wagon" on the board. Ask a child to exaggerate one thing like the story did (*example:* zebra and cart). The next volunteer might say "zebra and chariot." Compare your final phrase with the one on the board. Try other phrases like "bird with a worm" or "girl with a curl."

### Reading

After reading *Alistair in Outer Space*, distribute copies of the flying saucer on page 100. The children can write down six of their favorite books (books they would want to have with them on a long space journey). Compare the lists. Extension: As a homework assignment, the children can ask a grown-up to list some of their favorite children's books. Compare these as well.

## Books

Lester, Helen. *Pookins Gets Her Way.* Lynn Munsinger, illustrator. Houghton Mifflin, 1987. Pookins is used to getting her own way until she meets a magical gnome.

Mayer, Mercer. *Liza Lou and the Yeller Belly Swamp.* Aladdin, 1976. Liza Lou outwits some nasty inhabitants of the Yeller Belly Swamp.

McLerran, Alice. *Roxaboxen.* Barbara Cooney, illustrator. Lothrop, Lee & Shepard, 1991. A group of children create an imaginary town.

Pinkney, Brian. *Max Found Two Sticks.* Simon & Schuster Books for Young Readers, 1994. A young boy creates the sounds of the city after finding two twigs.

Sadler, Marilyn. *Alistair in Outer Space.* Roger Bollen, illustrator. Simon & Schuster Books for Young Readers, 1984. Alistair is kidnapped by aliens on his way to the library.

Seuss, Dr. *And to Think I Saw It on Mulberry Street.* Random House, 1972. Marco starts out seeing a horse and a wagon on Mulberry Street.

Soentpiet, Chris K. *Around Town.* Lothrop, Lee & Shepard, 1994. Describes some of the sights you might see on big city streets.

Steig, William. *Shrek!* Farrar, Straus & Giroux, 1990. Shrek is sent out into the world to discover his fortune and do his share of damage.

# Flying Saucer

Reproduce copies of the flying saucer for use with the reading activity on page 99.

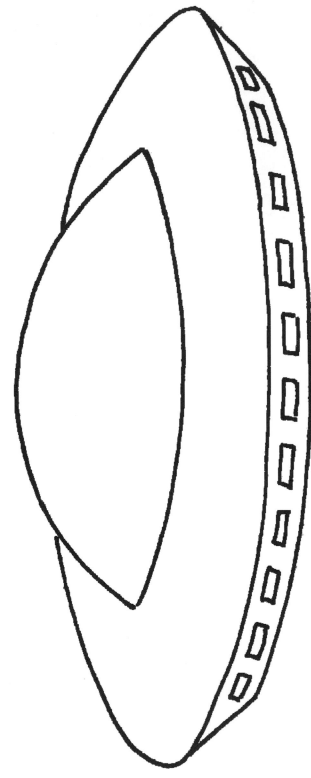

# 31
# Rub-a-Dub-Dub

Rub - a - dub - dub, Three men in a tub; And who do you think they be? _____ The but-cher, the bak-er, the can-dle-stick mak-er; They jumped in the tub to see where they could take her, So that's where they are you see. _____

**Original Lyrics**

Rub-a-dub-dub,
Three men in a tub;
And who do you think they be?
The butcher, the baker, the candlestick maker;
They all jumped out of a rotten potato,
So turn 'em out, knaves all three.

# Programming Ideas

**Theme:** bathtime

See Also: *Looby Loo (p. 91)*

## Setting the Scene

Talk about the things you do in the bathtub. Do you sing in the shower? Do you sing in the bath? Take an informal census of who likes showers more than baths.

## Song 🎵 *Rub-a-Dub-Dub*

Ask the children to name the three men in the tub from the old Mother Goose rhyme. If they can't, draw or give them hints (candle, cake, meat). Sing the song as it is given (not the original lyrics), then ask the children if they can pat the steady beat as you sing it again. Challenge them to try a harder pattern: Can they pat and then clap the steady beat? Challenge: Can they pat, clap, and push hands forward? Challenge: Can they pat, clap, push hands forward, and clap? Final challenge: Can they do it with a partner?

## Story 📖 *Rub a Dub Dub, Who's in the Tub?*

Make shaving cream drawings of the various inhabitants in the tub. Give each child a squirt of shaving cream the size of a tennis ball and let them draw on their desks or on a sheet of wax paper.

## Activities ✏️

### Reading

Read *Mortimer Mooner Stopped Taking a Bath*. Informally discuss cause and effect. Ask: "What happened when Mortimer stopped … cleaning his room? brushing his teeth? etc. What would happen if you stopped … cleaning your room? brushing your teeth? etc.

Extension: Chart weekly activities of school or home activities.

### Math

Graph of Showers vs Baths. Put two empty containers on a table. Using a ¼ cup of water to represent each child, ask them to place their ¼ cup of water in the category they use most. (*Hint:* Try using food coloring to have one color for showers and another for baths.)

### Art

Read *The Beast in the Bathtub*. Distribute the picture of the bathtub on page 93 and have the students draw their own imaginary beasts in the bath.

### Creative Writing

Write limericks featuring the three men in the tub. Possible prompts: "There once were three men in a tub" or "The butcher, the baker, the candlestick maker" *Or* suggest children write rhymes to explain why the three men were in the tub and where it would take them.

## Books

Arnold, Tedd. *No More Water in the Tub!* Dial, 1995. In an overflowing bathtub, Williams sails through the apartment collecting neighbors.

Conrad, Pam. *The Tub People.* Richard Egielski, illustrator. Harper & Row, 1989. The adventure of a family of wooden toys and near disaster of one in the bathtub.

Edwards, Frank B. *Mortimer Mooner Stopped Taking a Bath.* John Bianchi, illustrator. Bungalo Books, 1990. Mortimer refuses to do anything, including a bath, until grandmother arrives.

Oppenheim, Joanne. *Row, Row, Row Your Boat.* Kevin O'Malley, illustrator. Bantam, 1993. Starting off in the tub, a boy navigates through varied waters and ships.

Stevens, Kathleen. *The Beast in the Bathtub.* Ray Bowler, illustrator. Gareth Stevens, 1985. A young boy gets into mischief with an imaginary beast.

Takabatake, Jun. *Rub a Dub Dub, Who's in the Tub?* Chronicle, 1991. Bathtime becomes an adventure as creatures crowd the tub.

Wood, Audrey. *King Bidgood's in the Bathtub.* Don Wood, illustrator. Harcourt, 1985. No one can get the king out of his tub.

Ziefert, Harriet. *Harry Takes a Bath.* Mavis Smith, illustrator. Puffin, 1987. Harry takes a very messy bath.

# 32
# Sailing, Sailing

**Chorus**

Sail - ing, sail - ing, o - ver the bound - ing main, _____ For man-y a storm - y wind shall blow ere Jack comes home a - gain; Sail - ing, sail - ing, o - ver the bound - ing main, _____ For man-y a storm - y wind shall blow ere Jack comes home a - gain.

# Programming Ideas

**Themes:** ocean; weather

## Setting the Scene

Talk about the sounds you might hear if you were on a boat in the ocean: wind, waves, etc. Perhaps you could bring in a tape or CD of sea sounds. Discuss the weather and how it affects the sea.

## Song ♫ *Sailing, Sailing*

With the children standing, have them rock back and forth very gently to imitate the motion of a boat. Sing the song once. Have the children sway side to side. Sing the song. Then have them stand up very straight like a sailor with one hand in front across the stomach and one in back. Sway side to side and try to sing along.

## Story 📖 *Sail Away*

Ask: "What did the family in the story have to do when the weather changed?" Have children draw two pictures: a sailboat on the sea when the sky is clear and the sea is calm and one when the sky is cloudy and the sea is choppy.

## Activities ✏

### Science/Buoyancy

Read *How Do Big Ships Float?* Perform the What Floats/What Sinks Experiment: In a container of water, test the buoyancy of a variety of fruit and vegetables or other objects. Make a chart.

### Poetry

Discuss the sounds you hear in a boat (*examples:* wind blowing, waves lapping, motor humming, horns tooting). Write a haiku about sailing or boating.

### Research

List facts the children know about wind. Demonstrate the use of an encyclopedia. Look up "wind" and read the article. Add facts to the list. Then, with a fan, fabric and two volunteers, demonstrate how the wind changes a sail. (Note: This activity can be a good starting point for the concept of direction: north, south, east, and west).

## Art

Read *Banana Moon*. Draw and color pictures inspired by the book (*examples:* peach sunrises, candycane sails, tutti-frutti fish). Create a bulletin board or decorate the entire room. *Or* make suncatchers using the instructions below and the patterns on page 105).

### Suncatcher Instructions

*Materials:* Black or dark blue construction paper, tissue paper, scissors, glue stick, string or fishing line.

### Directions

1. Photocopy patterns for a template.
2. Fold construction paper and trace suncatchers onto paper. Cut along solid lines of each shape. Cut two copies of a pattern to make one sun catcher.
3. Place glue along the edges of one cut piece. Carefully place tissue over the glue. Glue edge on second piece and place on top. Trim tissue.
4. Pierce sun catcher in center and knot the line to hang.

## Books

Asimov, Isaac, and Elizabeth Kaplan. *How Do Big Ships Float?* Gareth Stevens, 1992. Gravity and buoyancy are explained.

Barton, Byron. *Boats.* HarperCollins, 1986. Different types of boats are explained.

Conway, Celeste. *Where Is Papa Now?* Boyds Mills, 1994. A young girl and her mother visualize the exotic places her father sails until his return.

Crews, Donald. *Sail Away.* Greenwillow, 1995. Follow a family's adventure at sea in a sailboat.

Garne, S.T. *One White Sail: A Caribbean Counting Book.* Lisa Etre, illustrator. Simon & Schuster, 1992. A counting book.

Ginsburg, Mirra. *Four Brave Sailors.* Nancy Tafuri, illustrator. Greenwillow, 1987. Four brave mice sailors fear only the cat.

Marshall, Janet Perry. *Banana Moon.* Greenwillow, 1998. Images are changed from food to tropical sights.

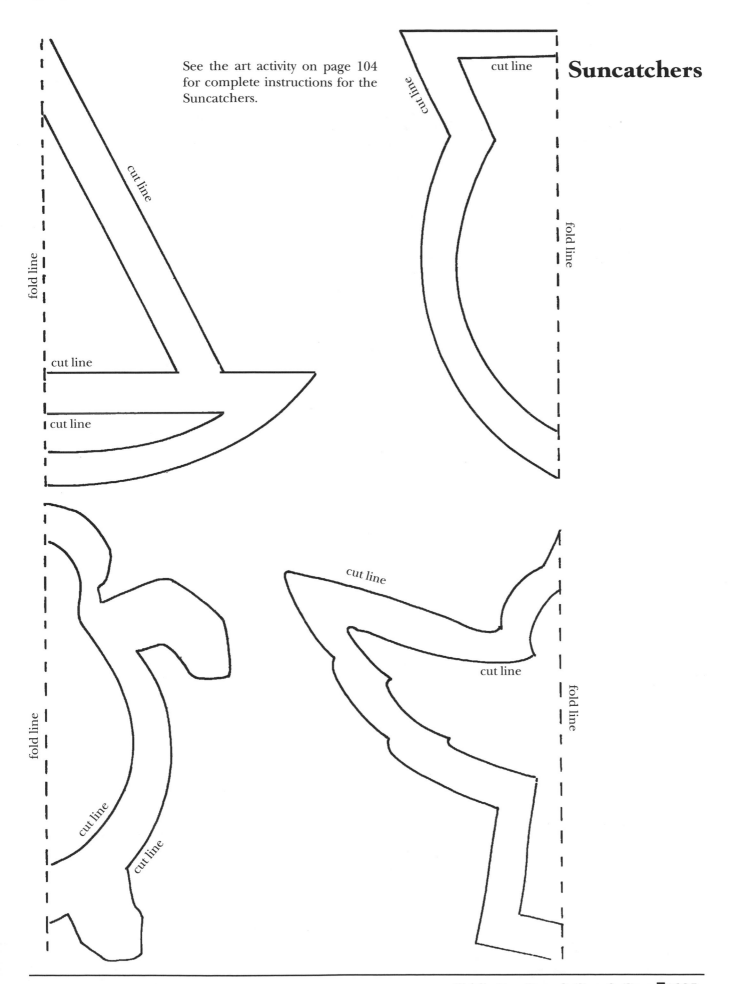

See the art activity on page 104 for complete instructions for the Suncatchers.

**Suncatchers**

fold line

cut line

cut line

cut line

cut line

cut line

fold line

fold line

cut line

cut line

cut line

cut line

cut line

fold line

# 33
# See-Saw Margery Daw

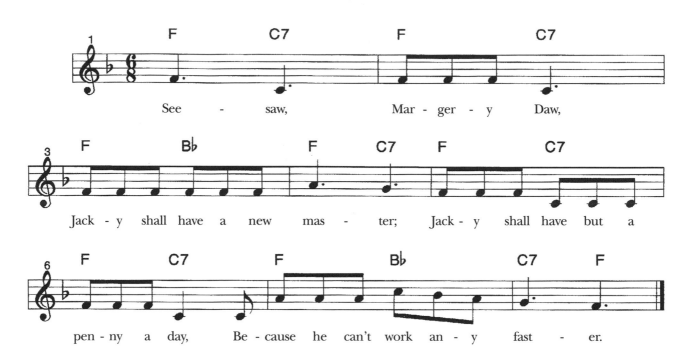

See - saw, Mar - ger - y Daw,

Jack - y shall have a new mas - ter; Jack - y shall have but a

pen - ny a day, Be - cause he can't work an - y fast - er.

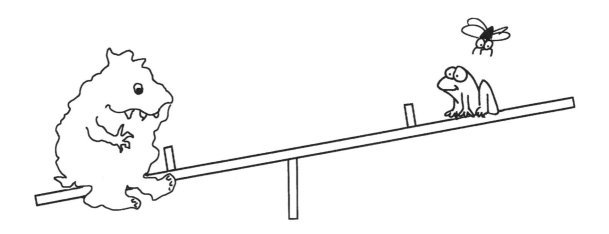

# Programming Ideas

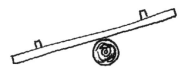

**Themes:** playing and play grounds

## Setting the Scene

Ask: "What kinds of things do you do on the playground at your school?" List the answers on the board. Vote to see which is the favorite at this point. Is there anything you would add to the playground if you could? Vote to see which would be the favorite now.

## Song 🎵 *See Saw Margery Daw*

Demonstrate a see-saw motion (arms extended out from your sides, when one goes down the other goes up) and ask the children to identify what you are. (*Hint:* You will find me on most playgrounds.) Ask for two volunteers to come up and stand on either side of you. When the left arm goes down, the student on the left squats down and when the arm rises, the student rises. The student on the right will follow the movements of the right arm. Once the motion is established, sing the song.

Ask for three different volunteers: one to be the see-saw and the other two to do the motions. Sing the song. Divide the class into groups of three and let everyone try it as you sing the song.

After singing, discuss the words. This is a children's song, but it may have originally been sung by men to help them keep the rhythm as they sawed wood.*

* Yolen, Jane. *Jane Yolen's Mother Goose Songbook.* Adam Stemple, arranger. Rosekrans Hoffman, illustrator. Caroline House, 1992.

## Story 📖 *Just a Little Bit*

Draw a see-saw on the board or put the drawing on page 108 on an overhead transparency. Write elephant on one side. Take suggestions for the weight of an elephant on the other. Demonstrate using an encyclopedia to find the average weight of an elephant. Were any of the guesses close? Read the book and find out how the elephant in the story was finally able to play on the see-saw.

## Activities ✏️

### Science

Read *Just a Little Bit* and use it as a starting point for a lesson on scales and measurements or simple machines. Reproduce the see-saw and animal pictures on page 108. Estimate weights or try to group animals so that their weights would balance. Look up weights in an encyclopedia and compare.

### Craft

Make see-saws using rulers and spools and create clay creatures to ride on them.

### Map Skills

Make maps of the playground. Ask students to add whatever they want to make the playground even better. (Extension: Read *Albert's Alphabet.* Ask: "Why would the principal ask Albert to create the alphabet on the playground. Do you like it? Why or why not?")

### Guidance

Read *King of the Playground* and discuss the story. Ask: "Has anyone ever dealt with a bully before? What did you do?" Ask children to respond (aloud or as an assignment) to situations given in the book or make up some of your own. Encourage them to come up with two answers: one serious and one humorous. *Or* read *Jim Meets the Thing.* Ask the children to list the things that frightened the characters. Ask: "Does anyone want to share something they are afraid of?" Discuss fear and what children can do when they are afraid.

## Books

Cohen, Miriam. *Jim Meets the Thing.* Lillian Hoban, illustrator. Greenwillow Books, 1981. Jim learns that everyone in first grade gets scared occasionally.

Gordon, Sharon. *Playground Fun.* G. Brian Karas, illustrator. Troll Associates, 1987. His friends figure out a way to help Billy the hippo have fun on the playground.

Naylor, Phyllis Reynolds. *King of the Playground.* Lola Langner Malone, illustrator. Atheneum, 1991. A young boy learns how to cope with the playground bully.

Pocock, Rita. *Annabelle and the Big Slide.* Gulliver Books, 1989. Annabelle slides down a big slide for the first time.

Tompert, Ann. *Just a Little Bit.* Lynn Munsinger, illustrator. Houghton Mifflin, 1993. A mouse and elephant need a lot of help before they can use the see-saw.

Tryon, Leslie. *Albert's Alphabet.* Atheneum, 1991. Albert builds the alphabet for a school's playground.

# See-saw and Animals

Reproduce the animals and see-saw for the science activity on page 107.

# 34
# She'll Be Comin' Round the Mountain

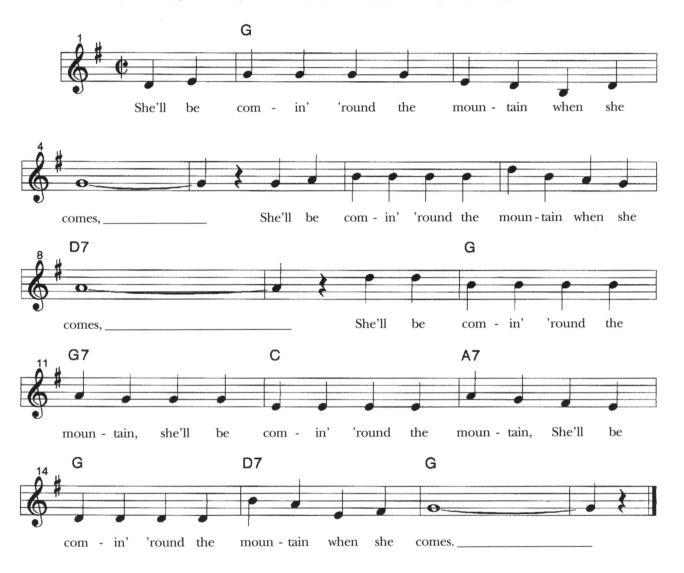

2. She'll be driving six white horses when she comes, etc.

3. Oh, we'll all go out to meet her when she comes, etc.

4. Oh, we'll kill the old red rooster when she comes, etc.

5. And we'll all have chicken and dumplings when she comes, etc.

# Programming Ideas

**Themes:** Appalachia; folktales

## Setting the Scene

Enlarge the prompt cards on page 111 so that each fits on a large sheet of paper. Post them across the board early in the morning without explanation. When ready for the activity, ask the children to identify the song and the words to the verses.

## Song ♫ *She'll Be Comin' Round the Mountain*

Ask five children to come to the front of the room. Hand each one a prompt card (enlarged from page 111). Review the words that match each card and sing the song.

## Story 📄 *She'll Be Comin' Round the Mountain*

Read the book by Tom Birdsey or one of the other versions listed in the Books section. As a class, in small groups, or individually, make up a new version. The version can be set anywhere in the universe, limited to a school setting, or tailored to fit another unit of study. (*example:* She'll be comin' round the island … driving six blue dolphins)

## Activities 🖉

### Craft

Read the author's note to *She'll Be Comin' Round the Mountain* by Tom and Debbie Holsclaw Birdsey. Use this book to launch a discussion on Appalachia. Read *Appalachia: The Voices of Sleeping Birds*. Using the pattern on page 112, make fans and decorate them with information or images they remember from the book. *Or* Read *Aunt Skilly and the Stranger* and design a classroom paper quilt (pattern ideas and instructions on page 113).

### Storytelling

Read *The Three Little Pigs and the Fox*. Discuss the oral tradition of folk tales. Reward any child who shares a folktale, original or otherwise.

### Dramatics

Read *Sody Salleratus* and encourage the children to act it out.

## Community Service

After reading *Silver Packages—An Appalachian Christmas Story*, ask the children to bring in money, toys or clothes they have outgrown. If it is the holiday season, wrap them in silver packages to give to more unfortunate children. Many charities will gladly accept such donations any time of the year.

## Books

Birdsey, Tom, and Debbie Holsclaw Birdsey. *She'll Be Comin' Round the Mountain*. Andrew Glass, illustrator. Holiday House, 1994. An Appalachian version of the traditional song.

Coplan, Emily, Doris Orgel and Ellen Schecter. *She'll Be Coming Around the Mountain*. Rowan Barnes-Murphy, illustrator. Bantam, 1994. A version of the traditional song.

Davis, Aubrey. *Sody Salleratus*. Alan and Lea Daniel, illustrators. Kids Can Press, 1996. A good read aloud tale where a squirrel saves a family that has been eaten by a bear.

Hooks, William H. *The Three Little Pigs and the Fox*. S.D. Schindler, illustrator. Macmillan Publishing Company, 1989. An Appalachian version of the familiar folktale.

Quackenbush, Robert. *She'll Be Comin' 'Round the Mountain*. J.B. Lippincott, 1973. A Wild West version of the traditional song.

Rylant, Cynthia. *Appalachia: The Voices of Sleeping Birds*. Barry Moser, illustrator. Harcourt Brace Jovanovich, 1991. Appalachia is lovingly described and pictured by an author and illustrator who grew up there.

Rylant, Cynthia. *Silver Packages—An Appalachian Christmas Story*. Chris K. Soentpiet, illustrator. Orchard Books, 1997. Every Christmas, a rich man throws silver packages from a train to the poor children of a community.

Stevens, Kathleen. *Aunt Skilly and the Stranger*. Robert Andrew Parker, illustrator. Ticknor & Fields Books for Young Readers, 1994. A woman and a goose scare a quilt thief.

Use these cards with setting the scene and the song activity on page 110.

# Story Fan

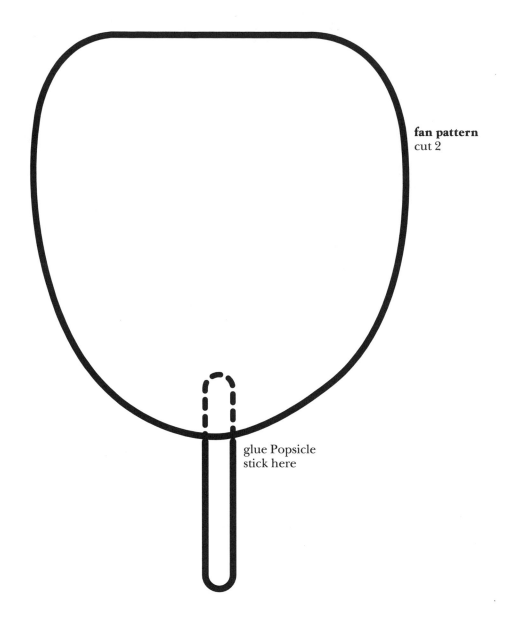

**fan pattern**
cut 2

glue Popsicle
stick here

## Fan Instructions

The fan is from the craft activity for "She'll Be Comin' Round the Mountain" from page 110.

*Materials:* poster board, scissors, glue, Popsicle sticks, and crayons or markers

*Directions*

1. Enlarge pattern and use as a template.

2. Trace fan template onto poster board and cut out (2).

3. Glue popsicle stick in place as shown in illustration.

4. Decorate fan with scenes from the story.

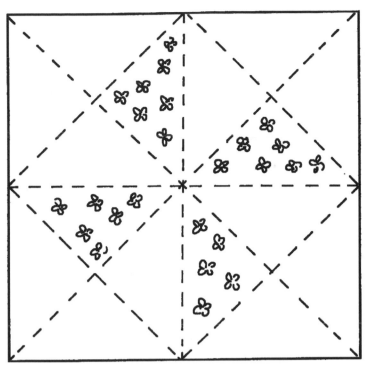

**Windmill design**

## Quilt Instructions

The quilts are from the craft activity for "She'll Be Comin' Round the Mountain" from page 110.

*Materials:* wrapping paper or wallpaper samples or construction paper, scissors, glue, and poster board

*Directions*

1. Enlarge patterns (Windmill/Bird in Flight) for an 8"x 8" template (or create your own).

2. Reproduce a template for each child and glue onto poster board.

3. Cut different patterns and colors of paper and glue them to the template. If children work on square independently, they may want to keep their square. Or, mount all the finished squares to form a group quilt.

**Bird in Flight design**

# 35
# Skip to My Lou

1. Fly in the but-ter-milk, shoo fly shoo!

Fly in the but-ter-milk, shoo fly shoo! Fly in the but-ter-milk,

shoo fly shoo! Skip to my Lou, my dar - ling.

**Chorus**

Lou, Lou, skip to my Lou. Lou, Lou,

skip to my Lou. Lou, Lou, skip to my Lou.

Skip to my Lou, my dar - ling.

2. Lost my partner, what'll I do?

3. I'll get another one, prettier than you.

4. Can't get a red bird, a blue bird'll do.

---

# Programming Ideas

**Theme:** movement

## Setting the Scene

Ask: "What are different ways we move?" List the answers you receive (*examples:* walk, run, skip). As a group, use a thesaurus and list synonyms for each word.

## Song ♫ *Skip to My Lou*

Make several blank blue ribbons. Hold an informal skipping contest. Ask for volunteers to demonstrate their skipping and award ribbons to each (*examples:* Highest Skipper, Funniest Skipper, Happiest Skipper). Conclude by playing or singing the song as everyone skips around the room.

## Story 📖 *Slender Ella and Her Fairy Hogfather*

Ask the children if they know what a hoe-down is. It was (and is) a time for people to get together for food, fellowship, and dancing. "Skip to My Lou" was a popular dancing tune (one that you might have heard at an old-time hoe-down). Read the book. Use a rhyming dictionary and come up with other kinds of godfathers (*example:* frogfather).

## Activities ✐

### Cooking

Read *Mirandy and Brother Wind*. Have a cakewalk with cupcakes for everyone. Extension: The children can split into pairs, come up with their own dance steps for "Skip to My Lou" and demonstrate their dances at the cakewalk.

### Creative Writing

Make up new verses to "Skip to My Lou." Give a prize to anyone who invents a dance or a game for the song.

Movement: Children have been skipping ropes for hundreds of years. Share jump-rope rhymes from *Anna Banana: 101 Jump Rope Rhymes* or different steps from *Jump! The New Jump Rope Book*. Have the children write down their favorite rhyme or challenge the children to write their own jump-rope rhymes as a concrete poem.

### Art

String Art. Make an art table or center. Put flat containers with different color paint, lengths of string, and blank paper on the table. The children take a string and wiggle it across the page or fold the paper in half over the string and pull the string out to create a picture.

## Books

Cole, Joanna. *Anna Banana: 101 Jump Rope Rhymes*. Alan Tiegreen, illustrator. Morrow Junior Books, 1989. Provides jump-rope rhymes for different styles of jumping.

Hurd, Thacher. *Mama Don't Allow*. Harper & Row, 1984. The Swamp Band enjoys playing at the Alligator Ball until they discover the intended ingredients of the main course.

Kalbfleisch, Susan. *Jump! The New Jump Rope Book.*. Laurie McGugan, illustrator. William Morrow, Inc., 1985. Presents techniques for jumping rope.

Lester, Helen. *Pookins Gets Her Way*. Lynn Munsinger, illustrator. Houghton Mifflin, 1987. Pookins is used to getting her own way until she meets a magical gnome.

Lyne, Alice. *A, My Name is…* Lynne Cravath, illustrator. Whispering Coyote, 1997. An alphabet book based on a jump rope rhyme.

McKissack, Patricia. *Mirandy and Brother Wind*. Jerry Pinkney, illustrator. Knopf, 1988. Mirandy tries to catch Brother Wind so he can be her partner at the cakewalk.

Oakley, Ruth. *Games with Rope and String*. Steve Lucas, illustrator. Marshall Cavendish, 1989. Games from around the world using rope or string.

Sathre, Vivian. *Slender Ella and Her Fairy Hogfather*. Sally Anne Lambert, illustrator. Bantam Doubleday Dell, 1999. A humorous version of "Cinderella."

# 36
# The Teddy Bears' Picnic

Music by John W. Bratton

# Programming Ideas

**Themes:** picnics; teddy bears

*The Teddy Bears' Picnic* is one of the few public domain children's songs that is not a folksong. We included it because we love the song and the teddy bear theme. Although it is a difficult song to sing, the children have a marvelous time moving to the music. The lyrics are available in Michael Hague's beautifully illustrated book entitled *The Teddy Bears' Picnic.*

## Setting the Scene

Ask: "How many of you have ever been on a picnic? What kinds of things did you do? What foods did you eat? Have any of you ever heard about the Teddy Bears' Picnic?"

## Song ♫ *The Teddy Bears' Picnic*

Have the children bring in teddy bears (see picnic idea below) or distribute teddy bear pictures on page 119 for the children to color and cut out. Play the tune or find a recording. (Bing Crosby, Rosemary Clooney, and Jim Kweskin and the Kids have all recorded the song). The children can move their bears to the music.

## Story 📖 *Where's My Teddy?*

After reading the story, talk about how Freddy felt alone in the woods. What was his surprise? Draw a picture of your teddy bear in the woods.

## Activities ✏️

### Craft/Writing

Make teddy bear picnic invitations for the teddy bears at home (or other stuffed animal if they don't have teddy bears). Invite the bears to come to the school for a teddy bear picnic (p. 119). *Or* use the picture as a writing prompt: "I love my teddy bear because…"

### Picnic

Have your children bring in teddy bears or bring in a few of your own. Have a picnic! Serve peanut butter and honey finger sandwiches and wash them down with berry juice (fruit juice). Take pictures of the picnic and the children with their bears. Talk about what bears do at night. After the picnic and the children have left for the day, have some bears spend the night in the room. Place them around the room engaged in various activities. Leave a note from the bears telling the children how much they enjoyed the picnic and party. The bears could leave their favorite recipe for porridge (instant oatmeal, raisins, and honey) which you could make in class.

### Movement

Read *Teddy Bear, Teddy Bear.* Act out the rhyme. If the children have brought in their teddy bears, the teddy bears can join in.

### Bulletin Board

Enlarge the Teddy Bear Invitation on page 122 to fit your bulletin board. Post snapshots of the picnic.

## Books

Alborough, Jez. *Where's My Teddy?* Candlewick, 1992. A small boy searches in the woods for his teddy bear and discovers a surprise.

Ets, Marie Hall. *In the Forest.* Puffin, 1976. A small boy's adventure with forest friends.

Hague, Michael (illustrator). *Teddy Bear, Teddy Bear: A Classic Action Rhyme.* Morrow, 1993. A colorfully illustrated version of the classic rhyme.

Hines, Anna Grossnickle. *The Greatest Picnic in the World.* Clarion, 1991. A family packs for the most delicious picnic only to have rain threaten.

Hissey, Jane. *Little Bear Lost.* Sandvick, 1994. Just when the picnic is about to start, Little Bear is missing.

Prater, John. *Once Upon a Picnic.* Vivian French, illustrator. Candlewick, 1996. Forest creatures are having a picnic while a family is having theirs nearby. Only the boy notices.

Kennedy, Jimmy. *The Teddy Bears' Picnic.* Michael Hague, illustrator. Holt, 1995. The Teddy Bears' picnic, illustrated.

Mahy, Margaret. *The Rattlebang Picnic.* Steven Kellogg, illustrator. Dial, 1994. The McTavish family go on a fun-filled picnic in their rattlebang car.

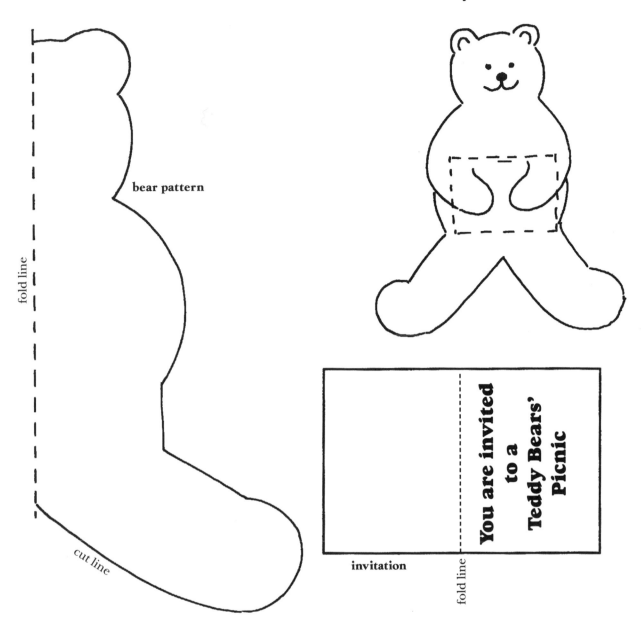

bear pattern

fold line

cut line

invitation

You are invited
to a
Teddy Bears'
Picnic

fold line

## Teddy Bear Invitation

The invitation is to be used with the song activity on page 118.

*Materials:* brown or tan construction paper, scissors, and a stapler

*Directions*

1. Photocopy bear pattern and use as a template. Place pattern on fold and cut.

2. Cut out invitation. Fold invitation in half and staple to bear.